Therapeutic Assessment and Intervention in Childcare Legal Proceedings

This book draws upon the author's first-hand clinical experience as an expert witness in child and family legal proceedings to explore the success of psychotherapy assessments and interventions. Focusing on families who are seeking to be reunited after the removal of their children into foster care, Mike Davies discusses critical aspects of therapy which can help to identify and engage those who will benefit from additional support.

Chapters combine heuristic, case studies and narrative research methodologies considering parents' stories, self-identity issues and assessment criteria to uncover an emerging framework that illuminates an innovative therapeutic approach. Divided into three parts, the book develops a comprehensive overview of and thorough investigation into therapeutic assessment during childcare legal proceedings, including explorations into crucial issues such as how and why some families are granted therapeutic intervention, as well as the level of understanding and expertise that professionals and local services can provide in these contexts.

Therapeutic Assessment and Intervention in Childcare Legal Proceedings will be key reading for researchers, academics and postgraduate students in the fields of child and adolescent mental health, law, social work and psychotherapy. The book will also be of interest to social workers, expert psychologists, psychotherapists, family therapists, psychiatrists and those specialising in public law.

Mike Davies is a Consultant Psychotherapist working in the UK, with expertise in child and family therapy and mental health.

Explorations in Mental Health series

Books in this series:

New Law and Ethics in Mental Health Advance Directives
The Convention on the Rights of Persons with Disabilities and the Right to Choose
Penelope Weller

The Clinician, the Brain, and I
Neuroscientific findings and the subjective self in clinical practice
Tony Schneider

A Psychological Perspective on Joy and Emotional Fulfillment
Chris M. Meadows

Brain Evolution, Language and Psychopathology in Schizophrenia
Edited by Paolo Brambilla and Andrea Marini

Quantitative and Qualitative Methods in Psychotherapy Research
Edited by Wolfgang Lutz and Sarah Knox

Trauma-Informed Care
How neuroscience influences practice
Amanda Evans and Patricia Coccoma

Learning about Emotions in Illness
Integrating psychotherapeutic teaching into medical education
Edited by Peter Shoenberg and Jessica Yakeley

The Philosophy, Theory and Methods of J. L. Moreno
The Man Who Tried to Become God
John Nolte

Psychological Approaches to Understanding and Treating Auditory Hallucinations
From theory to therapy
Edited by Mark Hayward, Clara Strauss and Simon McCarthy-Jones

Primitive Expression and Dance Therapy
When dancing heals
France Schott-Billmann

A Theory-based Approach to Art Therapy
Implications for teaching, research and practice
Ephrat Huss

The Interactive World of Severe Mental Illness
Case Studies from the U.S. Mental Health System
Diana J. Semmelhack, Larry Ende, Arthur Freeman, and Clive Hazell with Colleen L. Barron and Garry L. Treft

Therapeutic Assessment and Intervention in Childcare Legal Proceedings
Engaging families in successful rehabilitation
Mike Davies

Trauma, Survival and Resilience in War Zones
The psychological impact of war in Sierra Leone and beyond
David A. Winter, Rachel Brown, Stephanie Goins and Clare Mason

Therapeutic Assessment and Intervention in Childcare Legal Proceedings

Engaging families in successful rehabilitation

Mike Davies

Routledge
Taylor & Francis Group
LONDON AND NEW YORK

First published 2016
by Routledge

2 Park Square, Milton Park, Abingdon, Oxfordshire OX14 4RN
711 Third Avenue, New York, NY 10017

Routledge is an imprint of the Taylor & Francis Group, an informa business

First issued in paperback 2017

British Library Cataloguing in Publication Data
A catalogue record for this book is available from the British Library

Library of Congress Cataloging in Publication Data
A catalog record for this book has been requested

ISBN: 978-1-138-85664-6 (hbk)
ISBN: 978-0-8153-5846-6 (pbk)

Typeset in Bembo and Gill Sans
by Florence Production Ltd, Stoodleigh, Devon, UK

Contents

List of figures and tables

Figures

Tables

Part I

Background

Chapter 1

Expert witness or psychotherapist

A personal development account

'The happiness of your life depends on the quality of your thoughts'.
(Marcus Aurelius 121–180 AD)

Reflecting on development

Becoming a therapeutic Expert, especially one recognised in legal proceedings, raises issues about your self-identity in the role, as well as your perceived status and expertise. Further reflection on the meaning of this role naturally requires you to ask questions of where you professionally and personally locate yourself; what journey brought you here; what key influences have helped shape your identity; and what past learning and experiences still drive you. Reviewing my experience as an expert over the previous 13 years and more than 400 cases I have become increasingly aware of the personal and professional evolution that brings me to this point, and the many issues that were raised in relation to who and what I have become. These are issues of personal and professional identity in which I have been challenged to accommodate different roles that do not necessarily sit comfortably together. For example, I am a therapist, at times a practitioner–researcher, a consultant to organisations, and an Expert to the courts among other things. The roles, having some common ground, are not homogeneous and require some adaptability as you step in and out of a role according to the context. This is not an uncommon position to be in. However, the shift between therapist and Expert, referred to a little later in this chapter, is the most demanding I have experienced. It raises (and challenges), issues of self-identity, and the extent to which you are able to make compromises to accommodate the roles. It challenges your motivation and rationale for undertaking this role and is worthy of constant personal review to ensure your healthy psychological functioning.

The nature of self-identity is not necessarily static and may still be evolving with new experience and reflection. This is certainly the case with therapeutic identity, which I consider is still shaped by new experience and collaboration with others in particular. Reflecting on my therapeutic development I was never sure whether I was a therapist who saw individuals, but who liked working with families, or a family therapist who also liked working with individuals. I disliked the limitations of therapeutic modalities that prevailed for many years and which I felt stifled creativity – though this has significantly improved in recent times. I certainly crossed modality boundaries in search of additional tools and ideas, often because of expediency and the demands of very complex cases. The creative search for ideas and being innovative I hoped would benefit families who were invariably difficult to help. It was also a process that, on reflection, has enhanced my development.

I have spent the biggest part of my therapeutic career working with complex cases involving children and families in a variety of contexts. Working with marginalised, hard to help families in particular often requires innovation and flexibility on the part of the therapist and her/his agency. With this in mind I have gained experience and sought to be competent in different approaches, including: individual child-work, direct work with adults, working with parents or couple/family work and 'mixing and matching' as necessary – often alongside like-minded colleagues in order to meet a variety of need. While this is a challenging environment in which to work it is an opportunity to build a level and range of expertise that is an asset working in the context of legal proceedings.

Becoming an Expert

Without being able to pinpoint the time exactly, there was a stage when I was increasingly recognised as some kind of 'Expert'. It was somewhere between being a very experienced therapist manager, and then publishing research that lead to the development of specialist services for abused children. Because of the specialist nature of the work it naturally meant others came to me and my colleague who jointly led the service, for advice and consultation. A further development led to me giving evidence in court in relation to the complex cases referred to the specialist service. Leading the clinical development of this specialist team and providing consultation to others was the early preparation for the Expert role that was to follow. I enjoyed the consultative role but at that stage had no ambition to extend that to a court arena. The nature of working with abused children and their families/carers naturally leads to some court activity, which I undertook at that time on behalf of the service. As I gained experience I was increasingly asked to provide independent opinion on other cases outside of my clinical work.

The multiplicity of my clinical and research experience, alongside that of developing specialist services, and recent experience of giving evidence in cases of significant complexity, was the basis of my developing independent Expert status. The Law Society accepted me as an Expert in legal proceedings with children – something I had serendipitously become without any real ambition on my part. There are not many psychotherapists, who are not also psychiatrists or psychologists, who undertake Expert work, so I had no role model or framework to guide me. I was conscious of having to define who I was in relation to other Experts as well as the parameters of my expertise. I was also aware there are issues in relation to the Expert role including providing therapy in the context of legal proceedings.

There is a challenge concerning how you can truly incorporate the seemingly conflicting roles of psychotherapist and Expert in legal proceedings – without significant compromise. The legal context seeks 'truth' and certainty, while psychotherapy engages with the notion of several potential realities and unknowing. There are undoubtedly compromises to be made. Reflection and self-understanding are critical to your personal development as well as your well-being as you endeavour to accommodate both roles. As I gained experience I was increasingly motivated by the belief that psychotherapists have a great deal to contribute in legal proceedings, which benefits the legal process at times as well as families. Support for this is provided later in the case studies in Chapter 4.

I believe this view is supported by many of the professionals who work in legal proceedings who, despite being committed to the legal framework, also recognise its shortcomings in dealing with complex issues relating to children and families. Despite being (philosophically) diametrically opposed and potentially at odds with the legal system on many counts, psychotherapy and what it brings is often welcomed by other professionals, without completely understanding its value or relevance. In practical terms it seems to accept a certain amount of 'unknowing' so that it can pragmatically move cases on. In essence the professional/legal system is full of contradictions that paradoxically allow it some uncharacteristic flexibility at times.

The role of Expert is initially intimidating but also potentially seductive. It challenges your self-awareness and requires personal reflection, and high quality supervision. Your growing development in the role will benefit from feedback from others, including the agency commissioning your help, your peers, and most importantly your clients. I actively sought feedback from as many sources as possible from the outset. It is potentially seductive in that you can be treated with great reverence by other professionals – although beware, a good lawyer can also quickly undermine and expose the Expert who lacks caution and/or is unprepared. The term 'Expert' – not at all post-modern – is both a concept and a label that you have to accept and adjust to as it is unavoidable in the context of this work. Legal and other professionals will have expectations of you in the role beyond that of being a very experienced and competent psychotherapist. Establishing clarity about the parameters of your expertise in relation to each case as well as other professionals' expectations of you in the role is paramount. For example in a case where you have provided an opinion on the therapeutic viability of working with a family you may wish to comment more widely on the complexity of the case as you understand it. This is part of your role as an Expert and is often framed in your letter of instruction as 'anything else you consider relevant'. In my experience Experts deal with their role, and their perceived expertise in this context, very differently. Some are inclined to stay strictly within parameters while others are inclined to contribute more widely when they feel it is relevant. With the benefit of experience and growing expertise Experts perceive themselves, and are perceived by others, to have a particular identity in relation to their work. This is in part determined by your designation (e.g. psychologist) but also by your experience and generally acknowledged areas of known expertise (e.g. learning difficulties; substance misuse). Your self-identity as an Expert, and acknowledged areas of expertise, will naturally help shape the parameters of your assessment. It is also important to understand – and to be respectful of – the opinion and position taken by others in the case in relation to your own assessment, despite the adversarial nature of legal proceedings.

The role of 'Expert' in this context will be more challenging for some than others given many of the demands specific to the role. Perhaps a key capability, and a factor that concerns aspiring Experts more than anything else, is dealing with the process of being cross-examined on your own evidence as well as that of others. Being able to express your opinions clearly and revising them, if necessary, in light of new information while giving evidence, is demanding. In this respect having, or developing the ability to think on your feet when being cross-examined so that the best of your knowledge and expertise becomes available, is important in this role. Some Judges are more sympathetic than others toward the discomfiture of Experts when that occurs. There is often an expectation that you will contribute to untangling the complexity in cases so that the essence of the problems can be revealed and communicated in a way that is understood by lay or non-experts. Likewise there is often an expectation you will bring clarity to concepts such as 'attachment', 'good enough parenting', or emotional abuse so that they can be understood in more straightforward terms and related to the particular case.

While some Experts are very defined by their role (e.g. psychologist in learning difficulties or substance misuse) the role of psychotherapist requires a degree of systemic expertise – an ability to be almost constantly aware of the wider context in a case, particularly the impact of the professional/legal system, while also focusing on the specifics of the case. The demands made of you by others for information about some matter (e.g. depression) or for an opinion means the role is also more akin to that of being 'consultative' in other contexts – except here you may have to qualify your views and opinion via cross-examination at a later stage. The role of 'Expert' in legal proceedings, with all its inherent weaknesses, can be potentially transformative for some families affording a previously unforeseen opportunity for change. When the Expert (therapeutic) role is undertaken effectively the benefits of therapy – or the therapeutic approach – may not be just restricted to the family, but potentially make an impact with the professionals as well as the legal process.

The Expert experience

I first gave 'Expert' testimony in childcare legal proceedings in 1993 without realising I was doing so at the time. I was a manager of a multidisciplinary team of therapists providing specialist Child and Adolescent Mental Health Service (CAMHS) for abused children – called a Post-Abuse Service. In order to protect the therapists who were often very involved in direct therapeutic work with the children and/or families/carers I often took the responsibility for representing the work of the service in legal proceedings. If the therapist themselves gave evidence, then it could potentially undermine the therapeutic relationship and potentially sabotage work at a critical time. At that time we felt it was important for the therapists to feel they were free to get on with the work without these additional pressures. The other reason for me, as opposed to the individual therapist, giving evidence was, as I quickly learned, that most therapists are terrified at the prospect of giving evidence – it is very foreign, unfamiliar territory. I had experience of giving evidence in a previous professional life as a very young social worker and although apprehensive it was not completely unfamiliar – although the therapeutic versus the social work role was very different and proved to be a steep learning curve.

All professionals who give evidence have to lay before the court a summary of their qualifications, experience and areas of perceived expertise. Because I had, with a colleague, set up a specialist CAMHS for providing therapeutic assessment and intervention for abused children, their families and carers (largely based on my research and subsequent publications), I was increasingly perceived as an Expert and asked to consult with or give opinions in a variety of contexts including the family court. As I gained experience in the court system I was increasingly asked to give opinion on other cases, not only the Post-Abuse work. I did not enjoy the legal work and saw it as a necessity at that time. I resisted for some time legal work other than the Post Abuse cases I was committed to. At its worst you almost feel contaminated at times by the evidential process, especially the adversarial dimension. For a time I was prepared to do it so that Post-Abuse could function and although not enjoying the experience, developed some expertise along the way. Gradually, despite my concern with the system, I relented and undertook other expert work and was encouraged in this by others, especially lawyers and children's guardians. I also gained the view that a psychotherapy opinion was being welcomed in some cases and making a valuable contribution.

I really became an Expert by accident and despite its discomfort at times I was encouraged by the way it was possible to 'make a difference' with some cases that might not otherwise have been possible. Increasingly I became aware there were very few people with therapeutic expertise prepared to do this kind of work leaving the gap to be filled by clinical psychologists and psychiatrists – many of whom are not practising psychotherapists and therefore have limited therapeutic expertise. Over time I have developed my particular 'Expert' identity as someone who provides therapeutic opinion and where appropriate assists with intervention. I think it is reasonable to expect other Experts whose primary area of expertise is psychiatry, psychology or social work to comment on therapeutic matters. This is fine insofar as it enables the court to be generally more aware of important, very relevant factors in a case. However, where potentially life-changing decisions in a case may hinge on an assessment of significant therapeutic issues I believe this work should be undertaken by psychotherapists or other professionals who have significant psychotherapy expertise.

After leaving my specialist CAMHS position to work as an independent consultant I attracted a great deal of Expert work in family proceedings. I have always balanced this work with other clinical interests but I was able to undertake work of this kind on a much larger scale. With no established working framework or obvious role model for this work I discovered I had to find my own way. As I gained greater experience and developed expertise I asked questions of myself in this work, the demands of the Expert role, and the often desperate predicament of families caught up in legal proceedings.

I met hundreds of families for assessment and sometimes intervention during this time. This translates into hundreds of court appearances and more than a thousand reports, and of course many thousands of sessions with families. It was an intense, demanding experience during which I learned a great deal. Moustakas (1994) describes this as a 'lived experience' in which I had tacitly learned a great deal about the families, the system and therapeutic work in this context. I was aware by this stage that I had gradually established patterns of working and ways of understanding this work. Intuitively, the experience led me to develop a kind of framework that was guiding my activity in this work. The context, the case complexity, and the many dilemmas faced by a psychotherapist in this work presented many challenges. Asking questions of this experience and wanting to understand more was the motivation that led me to consider a research project. Alongside this I was struck by the potential for transformative change in a relatively small proportion of the families and the difference this made in terms of human and financial cost.

The Expert Psychotherapist dilemmas

Being an Expert and in a predominantly positivist legal environment implies a position of 'knowing' – as opposed to the position of most post-modern psychotherapists of being comfortable with 'not knowing'. In the words of Gilgun (2008):

> 'Not knowing means that we wait for evidence to come in before we draw conclusions.'

This suggests we can keep our options open and tolerate the uncertainty. He goes on to say:

'We continually look for evidence that adds to, contradicts, and undermines our evolving thinking.'

Gilgun suggests that in psychotherapy evidence is something that is constantly available for review, especially in light of additional information; and likewise opinion may be fluid reacting to evolving circumstances. On this basis you could argue that psychotherapists may be well suited to the legal arena – though in actuality it is often an uncomfortable, challenging environment that demands compromise. The court's search for truth or certainty is a challenging one for psychotherapists and many mental health professionals. In a sense the Expert psychotherapist's task is to take the opportunity to offer the court a perspective they would otherwise be unlikely to consider. While there is something of a natural ideological impasse here at times there is also the opportunity to offer a window on the world of the family, and an insight into their experience that the court might otherwise not have. In some cases it may also illuminate potential options (therapeutic intervention) for the family, worth trying before the court makes its final decision.

This challenge in some ways reminds me of the divide between the schools of quantitative and qualitative research methods and taking the findings obtained via one methodology into the camp of the other. That's what it feels like giving evidence sometimes. Squaring this circle (as an Expert) I have learned, demands you to be comfortable with yourself and the potentially conflicting role as you counter the expectations of Experts to provide certainty, facts and the (so-called) pursuit of truth. Given the multidimensional complexity in these cases, an attempt to reduce all too simplistic positivist certainty is illusory and provides an intellectual as well as philosophical challenge, not least when you provide a report or give evidence.

I have always been very uncomfortable with what I perceive to be the professional/legal system's adherence to a narrow child protection dogma – in a positivist legal context it can be at the expense of understanding underlying family problems that need to be addressed. This approach can lead to not only failing to understand but judging and condemning parents who are frequently trapped with overwhelming problems at many levels. At its worst it deals badly with families who are some of the most vulnerable in our society and who are essentially in need of help. I confess there have been times when I have felt frustrated and deeply saddened by the process at its worst. However, I have also had experience when the agencies and the legal system have demonstrated surprising flexibility – often motivated by genuine concern for the children and a willingness to meet their needs – despite all the limitations of the system. I do believe that Experts, and psychotherapists in particular, can have a positive influence on this process.

The 'Expert' role itself and the relationship with legal proceedings is full of contradictions and challenges. In my experience most professionals consider the legal system to be an unsuitable – and at times an oppressive – context for addressing complex child and family problems. The adversarial context inherent in legal proceedings can create as many problems as it resolves. The complex, multidimensional nature of the family's problems, often already caught up in conflict with Social Services, would benefit from 'meaningful conversation' to try and reach a more satisfactory resolution. The challenging nature of legal proceedings often stiffens parents' defensive resolve rather than encourages compliance and consensus. As positions become polarised and one side battles with the other, with each trying to win over the support of the Expert, the proceedings become protracted – sometimes lasting up to two years at considerable human and financial cost.

The adversarial legal template used in our family courts has obvious limitations and naturally struggles to resolve complex family problems. This often leads to cases becoming stuck for long periods in the legal process. The 'stuckness' is often mirrored in the relationships between some of the professionals and/or the parents. To a large extent the adversarial legal template exacerbates the problems and for a time becomes lost in the complexity. Apart from resorting to Experts for help, they have no other tool available to free up the process and may often be unaware of the nature of the problem. In my view it is at times such as these that Experts while understanding the complexity should also be able to take a wider view and understand the problems brought about by the process itself. This can potentially free up the process and make an invaluable contribution.

Despite all the serious limitations of the system I have experienced occasions when Experts provide opinions in a very complex case that has led to new understanding, allowing progress to be made. In some cases it appears that the complexity in the case is itself mirrored in the legal proceedings, thereby preventing progress for long periods. As cases unfold during the court process the complex multidimensional nature of problems – originally case-orientated but now layered systemically as a result of the professional/legal response – become more apparent. It is very easy to feel defeated in this environment. What has retained my involvement in this work and motivated me over the years is the potential for transformative change in some families – affording them an opportunity that may not otherwise have been possible. Although I am critical of the context of legal proceedings in many regards, and its potential impact on vulnerable families, paradoxically it offers some of them an opportunity for specialist therapeutic intervention, at a critical time in their lives, that they would not normally be able to access.

One of the perceived problems with the professional/legal system, and generally supported by a wide body of professionals (Kennedy, 2005), is the reliance on the adversarial element as a necessary aspect of law. The situation is already complicated by a variety of professionals, each with their own ideology and motivation attempting to resolve seemingly intractable issues in complex, multifaceted cases. The adversarial nature of proceedings does little to help this process and can exacerbate potential divisions rather than help resolve differences and reach consensus. While the legal system in this country makes some allowances in Family Law it is still an essentially adversarial system in which challenging cross-examination and winning the case are the principles that drive it. In this context 'prioritising the needs of the child' is a principle that loses out for a time to the dominating adversarial context inherent in the legal process.

It is no surprise when the family's complex dynamics not only become mirrored in the professional system but in the legal proceedings themselves. In a context such as this you can expect professionals from various disciplines to have different views of the family's functioning and their capabilities to care for the child. Unfortunately, as information becomes evidence so legal positions are taken up. In this context positions taken are often vigorously defended, becoming consolidated in the process. Like all conflict if not resolved early it has the potential of developing a life of its own and losing sight of its original purpose. In some cases it seems there is no 'right' solution, that whatever is decided will have serious consequences for the child. As Kennedy (2005) says it is sometimes a question of finding the least bad option in some cases, where the complexity and dilemmas faced are undoubtedly a challenge seemingly requiring the 'wisdom of Solomon'.

'Experts' at some stage are inevitably confronted with the limitations, and at times unsuitability, of the professional/legal system. The view that our current legal system is inadequate and often unsuitable for dealing with the complexity of family dysfunction and breakup is generally supported by 'Experts', having been debated in Parliament (*The Guardian*, 10 May 2011). Recent changes, mostly driven by cost, rather than the fundamental needs of the most vulnerable families in our communities, seem likely to only tinker with the system. More fundamental changes are required if we are to devise a system that more effectively balances the child protection needs of children on the one hand with the means to assist families with complex needs on the other. When fundamental change does come I believe most Experts hope it produces a system that is essentially aimed at reducing conflict and adversariality rather than one that depends on its existence to function in the first place.

The role of the independent Expert

The role of the 'Expert Witness' in childcare legal proceedings has been defined in the Public Law Outline (1 January 2008, see appendix i) in Practice Law Directions for Experts in Family Proceedings to: 'Provide an opinion that is independent of the party or parties instructing the Expert.'

As Justice Wall (2002) defined it 'the term Expert refers to persons external to the court proceedings and whom the court invites in, to enable them to advise on specific issues relating to the interest of the child'.

Many, but not all Expert witnesses are registered somewhere like 'The Expert Witness Directory' or the 'Consortium of Expert Witnesses'. There are others and they all have criteria for meeting their requirements for registration. This includes substantial qualifications and experience in your chosen field as well as publications and/or highly specialised expertise recognised by your peers and not readily available in mainstream services. Within your range of experience will usually include demonstrable expertise, witnessed and confirmed by others, in the role of providing assessments and producing reports and giving evidence in the court arena.

Most Experts in family proceedings prefer to take what are referred to as 'joint instructions' in which your particular expertise is recognised and agreed by all parties in the case. This at least prevents one party instructing one Expert against another, effectively taking away one level of potential conflict. The joint instruction means that all parties agree on your Expert status as well as the questions posed for you in the 'letter of instruction'. The 'letter of instruction' is the basis for your involvement and provides the parameters for your assessment and involvement in the case. Questions posed in the instruction can be anything from the very general: Does the father have a psychiatric disorder? or: Please provide a psychological assessment of the mother; to: Does the parent's historical substance misuse and domestic violence reflect an underlying personality disorder or relationship problems dating back to their own disrupted childhood experience? What would be the appropriate intervention and prognosis?

In most cases an Expert will receive a series of questions that often reflect the complexity of the case and the professional's need to understand the issues more clearly so that key decisions can be made. My assessments often follow the work of others who have identified a potential therapeutic issue that I have been requested to explore further. A typical question for a therapeutic assessment would be:

> Both parents have experienced adversity in their childhoods, with mother having been sexually abused as a child and father having been physically abused while in foster care. Father also has substance misuse problems that improved significantly since the children were removed to foster care. Are there therapeutic issues that can be identified and successfully addressed so that the parents can provide 'good enough' parenting for their children to be returned to their care?

Many Experts undertake the work as an extension of their clinical work and will expect the parents/families and whoever is to be seen to travel to them. Many, who like me cover a very large geographical area (up to 100 miles from my base), realise the logistical demands as being too great for most families. I have long since given up the 'secure base' of my clinic setting and more often than not travel to see families in their own locality using a variety of settings including: their solicitor's office; their own or a relative's home; or some acceptable neutral venue such as that provided by voluntary agencies like

'Barnardos' or 'Action for Children'. This kind of experience has enabled me to appreciate the value of seeing parents in a venue where they can feel relaxed and secure. Travelling to see a family means that you naturally have to allow time for the journey which can take a few hours each way. Over the years I have found this to be valuable time in which I mentally prepare for the case ahead, and on the return assimilate the experience and begin a process of reflection; all very valuable in the assessment process.

Professional context and the emergence of key questions

During the last 13 years working intensively with families in the context of legal proceedings I am struck by how their lives hinge precariously on the outcome of a professional's assessment of them. This is especially so with 'Experts'' assessments who often act as final arbiters on a family's viability, by providing independent psychological, psychiatric or social work assessments. Often psychological or psychiatric opinion is sought in relation to therapeutic matters although increasingly a small number of psychotherapists like myself now provide this service. A notable Expert witness and author of 'Psychotherapists as Expert Witnesses', Roger Kennedy (2005) describes 'being a so called expert witness in Family Law as carrying an awesome responsibility; recommendations made by the Expert may well help determine the future life of a child and their family.'

In my experience therapeutic issues and the nature of family problems in this context, are not well understood by many professionals. This sometimes leads to unrealistic expectations of the families and occasionally the provision of inappropriate and/or untimely interventions that are almost bound to fail. It is also true in many cases that where therapeutic issues are identified, that specialist intervention cannot be provided because local services either do not have the necessary expertise, or the service is unavailable at a critical time because of waiting lists, or a failure to meet their criteria.

My research study and this book have emerged out of this context and to some extent are inspired by the families who have successfully navigated legal proceedings and been reunited with their children. Knowing that some families are successful in this way begs the question – are there other families with potential for rehabilitation who are currently not recognised by professionals? Of equal influence have been the families whose circumstances are desperate and where highly skilled interventions are required whether or not they are rehabilitated with their children.

I have provided hundreds of assessments in the last 13 years regarding the potential viability of therapeutic work with families in the context of childcare legal proceedings. The life history of my involvement in these cases ranges from a month or two up to two years, where intervention is also provided. Sometimes after my involvement ceases they are re-referred for further work.

I have produced thousands of assessment reports and given evidence on hundreds of occasions. My identity in relation to other 'Experts' is clearly defined as someone whose expertise is not in psychiatric, psychological or social work assessments – but child and family therapy and related issues.

There are no statistics defining the number of cases whereby families are provided with therapeutic intervention during the course of legal proceedings. In my experience the number is relatively small. In some cases a therapeutic issue can emerge during proceedings requiring an Expert assessment before final decisions regarding the children are made. From my experience it seems serendipity is as influential as professional judgement, in determining which families compared to others get consideration here. For example, a change of the children's guardian in the middle of proceedings may lead to a different perception of the same case and highlighting previously unknown or dormant issues; or the emergence of new information which when uncovered throws new light on a case, for example: in a case where the parent discloses their abuse as a child during the proceedings, and wishes to engage with counselling. Questions are then raised about new therapeutic possibilities which may have an effect on the outcome of the case.

The work of childcare professionals in this context is guided by the Common Assessment Framework (CAF) – a generic assessment tool. There is no method or framework at this stage that helps signal for childcare professionals the potential need for therapeutic assessment and/or intervention, thus leaving a great deal to chance in these cases. According to Browne and Lynch (1996), it is questionable whether many social workers currently have the skills to identify families with this need – though from my experience many children's guardians do. Other Experts, including those in psychology and psychiatry who will have more knowledge of therapy, will not be guided by any framework specific to this context.

At present the literature on this subject is unable to guide us toward what helps or hinders therapy in these circumstances. The combination of case complexity, the challenges of the ubiquitous 'risk aversive' professional culture, and the sometimes intimidating context of legal proceedings, provide potentially overwhelming challenges particularly for the less experienced psychotherapist, psychologist or psychiatrist. During my research I spoke with many Experts who confirmed their fear of having made recommendations that were later perceived to have contributed to a very serious outcome for the child.

Some families at the stage of therapeutic assessment seize the opportunity and really engage in the assessment and subsequent therapeutic intervention, demonstrating they have the potential (not previously identified) to care for their child. Many, perhaps most of the families who reach this stage have severe and complex difficulties and may be unable to engage with help of this kind. Therefore it seems only a relatively small number of families are able to be rehabilitated successfully. The context of childcare legal proceedings is often a long, protracted and complex process resulting in major decisions about the children's future – often on a permanent basis. These are enormous decisions that have clear implications for the mental health and general well-being of the children as well as the parents and other family members. When family breakup occurs in this way and long-term or permanent decisions are made for the children there are still often ramifications as far as suitable placement for the child, and contact issues with birth family that endure beyond the completion of legal proceedings.

The process before and during legal proceedings is essentially adversarial (Brophy *et al.*, 2005) in which a great deal of information and indeed evidence is gathered about the family, especially in terms of 'parental deficits' and how this correlates with the 'significant harm' of the child(ren). Often attempts to address the parenting deficits and other problems will have already been tried by this stage and for a variety of reasons been unsuccessful. When making recommendations to the court my opinion will not necessarily be accepted, as there are often other views to consider; where it is, there is often a second stage of therapeutic and/or other intervention, as a final attempt to prevent permanent family breakup. The odds are often stacked against families successfully navigating these proceedings. Where there is still some potential in families that may be harnessed for a possible positive outcome for the children – given the enormity of the decisions – it is important that it is recognised by professionals and acted upon during proceedings.

References

Brophy, J., Jhutti-Johal, J. and McDonald, E. (2005). *Minority Ethnic Parents and their Solicitors and Child Protection Litigation.* Research Series 5.05. London: DCA.

Browne, K.D. and Lynch, M.A. (1996). 'A sad day for child protection'. *Child Abuse Review*, 5(2): 79–81.

Gilgun, J.F. (2008). 'Lived experience, reflexivity and research on perpetrators of interpersonal violence'. *Qualitative Social Work*, 7(2): 181–97.

Kennedy, R. (2005). *Psychotherapists as Expert Witnesses: Families at Breaking Point.* London: Karnac.

Marcus Aurelius, 121–180 AD.

Moustakas, C. (1994). *Phenomenological Research Methods.* Thousand Oaks, CA: SAGE.

Public Law Outline (2008). *Practice Law Directions for Experts in Family Proceedings*, 1 January, appendix i.

The Guardian, 10th May 2011.

Wall, N. (2002). 'Expert evidence 10 years after the implementation of the Children Act, 1989. Where are we?'. In: M. Thorpe and C. Cowton (eds), *Delight and Dole. The Children Act 10 Years On* (pp. 75–90). Bristol: Family Law.

Chapter 2

Context and review of the key issues

Parents, parenting and child protection in a risk-aversive culture

> 'The Tacit Dimension', we should start from the fact that 'we can know more than we can tell'.
>
> (Michael Polanyi, 1967)

Overview

A frequently encountered dilemma when constructing a review of this kind is to achieve a suitable balance between the general and wide ranging on the one hand and the specific on the other. This particular review is complicated because there is a dearth of (specific) literature available on this particular client group in this context. To offset this I have examined the themes and drawn from literature relating to families who encounter Social Services earlier in the process and prior to legal proceedings. As the literature points to these families as having severe wide ranging, multifaceted problems sometimes across generations, I have drawn heavily from the literature relating to dysfunctional families where concepts of 'significant harm', and 'good enough' parenting, and the issue of the children remaining in their care are central. 'Significant harm' and 'good enough' parenting are concepts originally described in the Children Act 1989 that are not only defined for the reader but explored in terms of its potential influence on the professional-client-professional relationship. Alongside the concept of 'good enough' parenting other, related aspects of parenting are considered, including parental breakdown.

When families become embroiled in legal proceedings, the professional–client relationship is widened to include those involved in the court proceedings with children, including lawyers of various kinds, a Judge or Magistrates, and a Children's Guardian. Further along the process various independent Experts may be commissioned to provide assessments. Therefore it seemed appropriate to make reference to not only care proceedings, as it forms a contextual backdrop, but the influence brought by the professional system dynamics. Parents' experience of proceedings is also briefly referred to as it potentially influences their ability to engage with the professionals who will ultimately decide the outcome of the case.

By the time the Local authority has embarked on the journey of legal proceedings they have already accumulated evidence they consider amounts to 'significant harm'. Moreover they will be engaged in establishing the parents are not 'good enough' and the children have been harmed by their behaviour and/or failure to meet their needs. These are children who will be considered to have been abused or maltreated as a direct or indirect result of their parents' care. The history and background to child abuse or maltreatment is referred to, so that the reader has an understanding of the ever-changing context as society's values and norms continue to evolve. Contemporary issues in relation to child maltreatment are also referred to so that the current context with all its inherent problems, for professionals as well as families, is illuminated.

Family functioning, parenting and child–parent relationships, especially when they malfunction, are also central issues. These families would be expected to have severe and complex problems that are often trans-generational in nature. This review draws on literature that enables the reader to understand these issues as they relate to the study, preparing the way for therapeutic and other interventions to be considered. Alongside this, the significance of 'early work and engagement' in assessment and therapy in this context is discussed. This is an extremely important theme running through this work.

A central theme of this study is 'relationships' in various contexts: relationships within families, between parent and child as well as parent to parent. The parents' relationship with their experience of being cared for will also be relevant. As a fundamental basis for understanding family relationship dynamics I draw heavily on attachment theory as a concept. It is referred to later as a major developmental theme as well as a significant influence as far as therapeutic intervention is concerned. Therefore attachment theory occupies an extremely important place not only in this review but in the framework and therapeutic approach referred to later.

Research on care proceedings

This is a highly complex and under-researched area (Brophy *et al.*, 2005). As a result there is currently a dearth of literature to help guide and influence the practice of those involved in this area of work, including Experts. A review of the research by Brophy *et al.* (2003) indicates a high use of 'Expert opinion' (89%) in cases brought to legal proceedings. Though there is an undoubted need for Expert involvement in complex cases, the evidence in this study suggests it is sometimes driven by the parent–professional and sometimes inter-professional conflict that arises. That activity involves a variety of Experts including the following: paediatric (filed in about 35% of cases); child and adolescent/family psychiatric (combining all types, filed in over 60% of cases); psychological (based on parents 24% of cases; based on children only, 14%); and psychiatric reports based on adults only (about 35% of cases). Cases also contain family centre assessments commissioned during proceedings (about 34%

of cases). Rarely are psychotherapists used despite the obvious need to identify or clarify therapeutic issues inherent in these cases. Historically in the vast majority of cases Child Psychiatrists, Psychologists, Independent Social Workers and Children's Guardians provide the bulk of the independent Expertise.

Research also indicates that most cases contain multiple categories of child ill-treatment and multiple allegations of failures in parenting. All applications contained serious allegations of maltreatment; less significant or borderline cases are not usually brought before the courts. Research also identifies that most children and parents are well known to local authorities. Indications are that cases that demonstrate an exception to this trend are likely to include those where there is evidence of a serious physical injury to a very young child with no previous involvement/concerns about parenting by Social Services. Further research on 'new/never known' families who become subject to care proceedings would be helpful in verifying whether there are other types of 'single event' cases and the profile of such cases. Similarly, further research would be helpful regarding the characteristics and other factors significant in families who successfully navigate legal proceedings with relatively positive outcomes. I can find no evidence in the literature of typologies of families or parenting styles that would indicate particular outcomes in legal proceedings. Any information that can potentially influence professional activity more likely to lead toward a successful outcome, or even reduce the time in legal proceedings with these cases, would therefore be welcomed.

Data on the socio-economic circumstances of parents requires updating as it relates to a period in the mid-1990s. However, the data at that time indicated most parents are struggling on the bottom rung of the ladder – over 80 percent were on income support at that point (Hunt *et al.*, 1999). With regard to specific concerns/allegations resulting in failures of parenting, research demonstrates most parents are highly vulnerable on several indices. For example, over 40 percent are likely to have mental health problems, many (20–30%) are likely to have drug/alcohol problems and many lead chaotic lifestyles (about 36%). Many mothers also endure domestic violence (45–50%); many parents (some 61% in the latest study) are reported to be unable to control their children. Half of all parents are also likely to experience housing problems (Brophy *et al.*, 2003; Hunt *et al.*, 1999; Bates and Brophy, 1996). In addition to the above features, most applications (over 70%) also include allegations regarding the failure of parents to cooperate with welfare and child health professionals (Brophy *et al.*, 2003). This is clearly a significant characteristic associated with these families but in my view exacerbated by the legal, or impending legal process. These demographics are indicative of significant problems with individual and family functioning affecting the well-being of children. There are undoubtedly a range of therapeutic and other interventions and support that families will benefit from in these circumstances. Whether addressing therapeutic issues is potentially significant in the outcome for these families, including whether they are timely and appropriate, is not clear from the review, but is referred to later in this book.

Brophy *et al.* (2005) also suggest two main areas for consideration resulting from their study. Firstly there are multiple vulnerability factors in the profile in almost all parents and children in these cases; secondly, the need to explore current and prospective harm, and in many cases a need for dual diagnosis, indicates case complexity, and the need for clinical (as well as social work) input.

Clinical skills and opinion, as part of the evidence, are likely to be required; for example to address the aetiology of the child/ren's problems/difficulties/injuries, and to arrive at a prognosis about future harm, as well as the child/ren's needs and parental capacity for change. I support the use of Experts in this context as the nature and level of expertise required in these complex cases is at times beyond that of any single professional discipline, including social work.

These factors are likely to make case profiling and defining typologies of parents, which may lead toward some kind of predictive model in this context, very difficult to achieve. In many of these cases a great deal hinges on the Expert opinion in such matters.

The study by Brophy *et al.* (2005) indicated the vast majority of cases have such complexity they found it necessary to utilise Expert evidence in at least one form. While there were some regional differences, many cases are likely to require knowledge, skills and diagnostic and prognostic expertise beyond those usually found in social work. In general, expert opinion is accepted by the court, often playing an influential role, even though the recommendations made may not always be followed. However, in a minority of cases where there is unusual complexity, and/or new issues arise, a second Expert opinion is sought on the same matter. According to Brophy *et al.* (2005) in most areas there is a shortage of available Experts prepared to undertake this work and it is one of the reasons proceedings can take so long to complete. Arguably this situation has recently been exacerbated by government changes to the funding arrangements following which many Experts have made themselves unavailable.

Placement of children back home with their parents was less successful (41%) compared to adoption (58%) and kinship care (78%) and foster care (68%). Foster care inevitably became the collecting ground for children who had often had a range of placements that were unsuccessful (Harwin *et al.*, 1999). The figures themselves do not tell the whole story of course. Often sibling groups are broken up and difficult to place. Families who have children returned to their care are not necessarily supported and provided with the help they require so that the rehabilitation can be sustained long term. What is also not shown in the figures is that services are not geared toward supporting families with rehabilitation, or indeed supporting vulnerable families long term, where that is necessary to prevent family breakup in the first place. Farmer *et al.* (2011) in their recent study found inadequate social work planning, assessments and support of families who were 'reunified' as being associated with breakdown.

They followed up to 100 children (two groups of 50) and compared successful and unsuccessful groups of children up to 14 years of age to identify what factors were associated with a successful outcome. Interestingly they are similar factors to those associated with fostering and adoption breakdown (Sinclaire, 2005). Her study also indicated younger children under 11 years had better outcomes than older children especially when they had been in care for an extended period. The research also points to addressing a range of significant parental problems such as alcohol and drug misuse, and parenting skills. Parents reported they wanted help with problems of substance misuse, child management skills, as well as direct help (mental health) for children. Interestingly the parents also felt they would benefit from help that 'built up their confidence as parents' and to be 'listened to and respected'. This indicates a relationship dynamic issue that is not explored in any depth in the study. There is no mention of therapeutic work although it recognises the need for specialist support services including mental health. As I read the book, seeing the issues through my particular lens, it appeared to me that many of the issues required a therapeutic focus. In fairness theirs was not a therapeutic but more general focus on issues affecting reunification.

Parents' experience of proceedings

Here again there is very little research although the difficulties of obtaining views of parents and children in this context are recognised. However, a study by Freeman and Hunt (1998) indicated parents would prefer a less formal environment, and while in the courtroom they would feel better sitting next to their lawyers. The legal formality and general environment, although reduced in family law, still engendered a sense of criminality for most parents. However, most parents felt positively about Judges but less so with Magistrates (Freeman and Hunt, 1998). This may well be down to what is commonly referred to as 'Judge-craft'; but also, relating to a single person in the form of a Judge, during proceedings, compared to three Magistrates, is also thought to have distinct advantages. It is also accepted wisdom that a Judge, in comparison to magistrates, will have greater expertise and gravitas in dealing with the whole care proceedings process. Parents clearly felt better when Judges talked directly with them as issues arose, and in involving them appropriately during the proceedings. Parents also needed the translation of many of the legal, social work and other professional jargon and naturally felt the use of more straight-forward language would have helped them. Some parents wanted more Judges and Magistrates from minority ethnic backgrounds (Brophy *et al.*, 2005). Although there is only limited research it indicates how parents feel, not only alien in this context, but disadvantaged by their lack of education and ability to understand what is happening at times.

Important aspects of parenting

Jones (2001) when referring to parenting describes activities on the part of the caretaker that lead to the child becoming autonomous. Reder, Duncan and Lucey (2003) go further describing the 'purpose of parenting is to facilitate the child's optimum development within a safe environment'. Hoghughi (1997) describe core elements to parenting:

- Care (meeting the child's needs for physical, emotional and social well-being and protecting the child from avoidable illness, harm, accident or abuse);
- Control (setting and enforcing appropriate boundaries);
- Development (realising the child's potential in various domains);

Then describing parental qualities he refers to:

- Knowledge (how the child's care needs can best be met, the child's developmental potential, how to interpret the child's cues, sources of harm);
- Motivation (e.g. to protect, to sacrifice personal needs);
- Resources (both material and personal); and
- Opportunity (e.g. time and space).

Hoghughi (1997) also describes how 'qualities and key facets of parenting need to be achieved in an evolving relationship between parent and child and where the context may well change. In this the child is not perceived as a passive recipient of parenting nor is the parent a mechanical or ubiquitous provider'.

Quinton and Rutter (1988) see parenting as 'not only what parents do with their children and how they do it, but also something to be affected by the quality of the parents' relationships, by their psychological functioning, by their previous parenting experiences of parenting other or a specific child, and the social context in which they are trying to parent'. Parental competency is obviously a key component in facilitating and enhancing parent–child relationships. Belsky and Vondra (1989) noted from an extensive study that parental competence is multiply-determined and that factors are interrelated, but that the parents' personal psychological resources are most crucial. Schaffer (1998) agrees that 'no single attribute of the child, parent or family determines the quality of the parenting relationship, since it is multidetermined'. Furthermore, Golombok (2000) as well as Schaffer (1998) conclude that family structure or individual parental attributes matter far less to children's development than the quality of relationships within the family and the wider social world.

'Good enough parenting'

'Good enough' parenting like significant harm is socially constructed and relates very much to the accepted parenting norms of the day. Woodcock (2003) studied the Judgements of child protection workers to understand what constituted 'good enough' parenting. She included in her list: capacity to prevent harm; capacity to recognise the need for and provide supervision; capacity to provide routine and consistent care; emotional availability and sensitivity and insight into the reasons for the child's behaviour; a level of affect and interest in the parent–child interaction; and finally, not resisting professional expectations about their parenting.

This last item is very important and can determine the quality of the working relationship between professional and parent. Azar and Cote (2002) question how appropriate such professional parenting standards are when there are many in the general population who would not have the capacity to perform some or many of these tasks to the requisite standard. This indicates that serendipity may be a factor in which some families, who meet the criteria for concern, are referred for investigation, while clearly there are many that are not. Many families rather than focusing on the concerns which are raised about their care of a child, tend to justify their behaviour and/or standards by comparison with other families in their community.

However, Budd (2001) makes a very valid point when referring to the perceived higher standards expected of parents trying to retrieve their children from care. The threshold for 'good enough' parenting seems to have been raised to a new level, higher than other parents in their community, as well as being higher than the level expected of them, prior to the child's admission to care. There is undoubtedly a variation in expected standards among child protection workers of what constitutes 'good enough' parenting capacity in many areas. This also appears to be determined by what stage in the process the case is in at that time: whether at the point of child protection investigation, or already in legal proceedings, or when considering rehabilitation.

Daniel (2000) noted the importance of workers making explicit their values that underpin their assessments, noting how different kinds of emphasis by workers may result in very different thresholds for removal. Fook et al. (1997) point to the absence of a specified framework for decision making, finding that even experienced social workers are often unable to articulate the reasons behind recommendations they have made.

It is very easy to be critical of child protection workers who, as Shlonsky and Wagner (2005) point out, have to weigh up and prioritise information without the benefit of a framework. They also indicate the potential for irrelevant factors becoming influential in the assessment without a guiding decision-making framework. However, there is clearly potential for subjective elements to be influential in the assessment process, including the prospect for establishing a working relationship between professionals and parents.

It is not only child protection workers who have problems with assessments of good enough parenting. Budd (2001) raised concerns about the accuracy and validity of psychometric tests often used by clinical psychologists. However, the findings of psychologists and psychiatrists are afforded greater value than those of experienced child protection workers, who have been involved with the family over a much longer period. Risley-Curtis *et al.* (2004), Budd (2001) and Azar *et al.* (1998) agree that many reports (including Expert) are of variable quality. This is very much in line with my personal experience. In particular I am concerned about what I consider to be the overemphasis on psychometric data obtained by clinical psychologists in their assessments.

Woodcock (2003) found that social workers rarely referred to psychological evidence. Referring to earlier work by Parton *et al.* (1997) she refers to a 'surface-static notion of parenting where there is a failure to address psychological factors underlying parenting problems even when they have been previously identified'. Also identified was the tendency of social workers to rely on 'exhortation to (parental) change', rather than a response informed by psychological observation. When parental change did not occur, in many circumstances it was often perceived as resistance.

In such cases it appeared the social workers felt the parents were locked into their behaviours, seeing this as a personality trait and deeply ingrained. Although at odds with the psychological literature on parenting, social workers in the study appeared intent on 'getting the parents to change'. They see 'parental change' in these terms and 'accepting responsibility' as the core to providing good enough parenting in many cases often at the detriment of focusing on the multiplicity of problems that beset their parenting (Woodcock, 2003). I think this aspect of the research is very important and fundamental to the failure or otherwise of the parent–social worker relationship. This kind of approach by social workers can frequently be the basis for a spiralling conflict which inadvertently prevents meaningful dialogue between them. On the theme of social work practice being informed by the literature, Risley-Curtis *et al.* (2004), refer to a lack of dissemination of mental health journal material to caseworkers. Social work decisions seem to be more influenced by legal and quasi-legal decisions in a context whereby 'practical reasoning' was a favoured approach (Parton *et al.*, 1997). I would add that social workers' understanding of therapeutic issues – a close first cousin of 'underlying psychological difficulties' – is variable and often poorly understood.

In an attempt to establish some areas of agreement Teti and Candelaria (2002) in their comprehensive review of parenting competences, noted that successful areas included parental warmth, sensitivity, and acceptance of children's basic needs. These were the core features associated with positive outcome irrespective of age, temperament and general resilience. Although control was also a key competence, warmth and sensitivity is a more influential factor than control without warmth.

Azar and Cote (2002) identify the key parenting competence as 'adaptability'. The need to adapt flexibly to the changing circumstances and requirements of family life can only occur with accurate problem-solving and accurate perception of a child's capabilities – pointing again to the significance of a parent's underlying psychological profile.

In line with this view of adaptability being a key component Azar *et al.* (1998) suggest the significance of being flexible, without becoming rigid, especially as stages of child development and the family life cycle unfold. They suggest that as the child grows in competency through the developmental stages, so also do the parents as the family evolves and develops.

Cann (2004) introduces the notion of reflective parenting as an indication of competency. In this, parents demonstrate a capacity to question their skills and abilities in light of experience, providing a kind of self-review of their parenting.

There is often widespread disagreement on parenting issues as witnessed in the many debates that have taken place on corporal punishment. Even Experts have discrepant views regarding the benefit gained or damage incurred to a child when 'smacking'. There is a complex relationship between advances in knowledge, public opinion and legal changes (Roberts, 2000). Conventions and legislation concerning smacking or corporal punishment and our attitudes to children vary considerably across cultures. It is also erroneous to believe that public opinion will naturally follow legislative change, as some attitudes remain persistent in large sections of society (Roberts, 2000). This leaves open the potential for conflict between some sections of the community and those representing authority on controversial matters such as what constitutes child abuse and what is reasonable chastisement. I think this is very important and may explain why families in marginalised communities have values that underpin their approach to parenting that may be markedly different and lagging behind changes that have already taken place in mainstream society.

Assessment of parenting breakdown

As a means to developing a framework for understanding and intervening in family crises many authors have discussed assessment of family breakdown, including Steinhauer (1983), Bentovim *et al.* (1987), Sturge (1992), Tufnell *et al.* (1996), Glaser (1993), Wolkind (1994), Iwaniec (1995), Herbert (1996), Budd and Holdsworth (1996), Kennedy (1997), Black *et al.* (1998), Sheldrick (1998), Azar *et al.* (1998), Howe *et al.* (1999), and Jones (2001).

In addition some authors, namely Oates (1984), Swadi (1994), Gopfert *et al.* (1996), Jacobson *et al.* (1997), Henry and Kumar (1999), Jenuwine and Cohler (1999) and Drummond and Fitzpatrick (2000) have focused on parenting of adults with mental health and/or substance misuse problems. Many of the families who find their way to legal proceedings will have substance misuse problems and/or mental health difficulties.

Reder *et al.* (2003) interestingly brought together contributions from psychologists and psychiatrists involved in childcare legal proceedings. In all of these studies a range of styles is represented. Kennedy (1997) has referred to psychoanalytic principles as important in understanding family breakdown. Howe *et al.* (1999) uses attachment theory to postulate on parents' 'internal working model' of self and others to assess parental functioning. Azar and Weinzier (2005) refer to using cognitive assessment to understand parent competency and also referred to matching the specific needs of the child with the level of parental competency required for that particular child's needs in what they term a 'functional-contextual perspective'. His main categories are: Parenting (child management); social cognitive (problem-solving); self-control (impulse control); stress management (coping capacities); and social (e.g. empathy).

He further recommended assessing factors relating to: the parent; the child; parent–child interaction; and systemic issues.

I think each of the approaches and therapeutic positions recommended have relevance for families who find their way to legal proceedings. However, these are complex cases with a multiplicity of need that often require a multi-dimensional approach to achieving the necessary change.

Child maltreatment

History and background

Maltreatment of children by their parents or other caregivers is a major public health and social welfare problem in high income countries. It is common and can cause death, serious injury, and long-term consequences that affect the child's life into adulthood, their family and society in general. Every year four to 16 percent of children are physically abused and one in ten is neglected or psychologically abused. During childhood, between five percent and ten percent of girls and up to five percent of boys are exposed to penetrative sexual abuse and the number increases threefold if you broaden the definition of sexual abuse to include other sexual experiences. However, substantiated incidents of maltreatment amounted to less than one-tenth of these statistics. Long-term problems for the child include mental health, substance misuse, risky sexual behaviour and criminal behaviour (Gilbert *et al.*, 2009).

The notion of 'child abuse' or 'child maltreatment' has been developed in relatively recent times and in the higher income West (Gilbert *et al.*, 2009). Arguably child abuse became more generally recognised when Kempe *et al.* (1962) invented the term 'battered child syndrome'. It caused a stir at the time, made more so because it produced medical evidence to substantiate claims that parents caused severe harm and even death in some instances to their children. For the first time there was believed to be a 'scientific basis', not only identifying cases of maltreatment of children, but by implication – state intervention in family life to safeguard children where necessary. As paediatric expertise grew in this area, society (at least in the West), could not ignore the evidence, and the basis of modern child protection agencies and eventually formalised procedures to guide multidisciplinary activity was born.

You could be forgiven for thinking that abuse and maltreatment of children is therefore a modern phenomenon. This is not the case and there is evidence that some children have endured quite appalling treatment often from their own families, throughout history and across cultures and ethnic groups. The development of concepts relating to children's treatment in this regard and intervening in families where children are at risk is a recent phenomenon and far more developed in the higher-income West.

Concern for children's welfare in a more coordinated fashion began in this country during the industrial revolution. Some philanthropic, often middle-class individuals became alarmed at the large numbers of destitute children in the new cities and towns that had developed during the industrial revolution. It also became apparent that some parents were not or could not fulfil their duties to the child and were even exploiting them in some circumstances. So the notion of families not providing good enough care, and consequent state intervention in family life to make children safe, was gaining ground. Concern for children's welfare grew during the 19th century much of it via well-intentioned voluntary activity intending to safeguard children and protect them from harm and exploitation.

Concern for children's welfare continued throughout the 20th century in which the world wars had a profound effect on families. The Second World War in particular led to many children being separated from their parents for long periods of time or even orphaned in many cases. There was societal concern for large numbers of children who were traumatised by experiences and/or affected by separation and loss. This brought into sharp focus children's emotional needs and the development in this country of post-war local authority-based (as opposed to voluntary) welfare organisations, including children's departments created especially to be concerned for children's welfare.

Recent developments and the 'risk aversive' culture

By the time of the children Act 1989 and the subsequent 'Working Together' document there were four categories of child abuse in this country: physical abuse; neglect; emotional abuse; and sexual abuse. Alongside this, new concepts emerged such as 'significant harm', 'good enough parenting', and the 'needs of children being paramount'. The 'Working Together' document that followed also laid down guidelines for multidisciplinary professional practice for the first time. 'Significant harm' was introduced in the Children Act 1989 as the threshold that justifies compulsory intervention in family life in the best interests of the child. Significant harm refers to any physical abuse, sexual abuse, emotional abuse and neglect, whether by accident or injury and attributable to lack of parental care or control, that is sufficiently serious to adversely affect progress and enjoyment of life (Adcock, *et al.*, 1991).

Harm itself in this context is defined as the treatment or impairment of health and development (Working Together, 1989). Importantly there are no absolute criteria on which to rely when judging what constitutes significant harm. Sometimes a single violent episode may be considered sufficient to constitute significant harm but more often it is the accumulation of significant events, both acute and long-standing, which interrupt, damage, or change the child's development.

Suspicions or allegations that a child may be suffering significant harm can be enough to trigger a Section 47 (child protection) investigation (*Children Act 1989*) into a family's life. This is often the first stage of involvement with Social Services for some families.

The problem with the concept of 'significant harm' and 'good enough parenting' is that they are all ultimately socially constructed terms (Reder *et al.*, 2003). They depend on someone's subjective impressions, culture-bound beliefs (Maitra, 2003) and context-related thresholds of concern, as much as objective qualities (Dingwall *et al.*, 1983). This is further complicated by the evolving nature of child abuse where society's approach to this emotive subject fluctuates; guidelines are constantly reviewed and amended and continue to be influenced by very serious child protection inquiries that have arisen often following the death of a child and where professional activity, or the lack of it, is perceived to have failed to avert a disaster. Public as well as professional perception of agencies' failures and constant changes in procedures, and unrealistic expectations and pressure on social workers create an insecure base for professionals working in child protection. This kind of intense pressure on professionals inevitably influences their activity with the families as well as the relationships they develop.

Platt (2008) used qualitative methods to explore the effects on the parent–social worker relationships of more or less coercive interventions in the context of child protection. It discovered that less coercive interventions were associated with better relationships but were not necessarily a pre-requisite. They also found that a worker's skill was also an influential factor.

In a recent review by Turney *et al.* (2011) they indicated the relationships formed between social workers and parents during assessments serve a dual function of allowing the work to proceed, at the same time as providing relevant information. They recognised it is not always easy to establish 'good partnership' or 'cooperative working' and there is a degree of consensus about the characteristics of 'hard to help' parents (Hindley *et al.*, 2006; Thoburn *et al.*, 2009). Most importantly, the research does not identify clearly the extent to which parental involvement and cooperation is affected by the knowledge and skills of the social worker compared with other contributory influences, especially the attitudes and behaviour of the parents, and also the organisational or managerial systems within which practitioners work.

The relationship between parental engagement and outcomes for children remains under-researched. However, there is considerable evidence that the nature of parental relationships with professionals affects decisions arising from assessments (Brophy *et al.*, 2005; Cleaver *et al.*, 2004; Holland, 2009; Iwaniec, 2004; Masson *et al.*, 2008; Platt, 2008; Wade *et al.*, 2010). Other research evidence points to practitioners becoming 'enmeshed' in chaotic family systems (Brandon *et al.*, 2009) and find their attention diverted away from the child by needy parents.

It is often an intense and highly emotive context; emotional on the part of families because they are defending their viability as a unit, their very survival together may be dependent on the outcome of an investigation or assessment; but also emotive and highly pressured for professionals and their agencies, who fear repercussions if they are perceived to have made a mistake – one that ultimately led to a disaster. When this happens, the media and to some extent professional bodies, are unforgiving toward professionals perceived to have erred. This has led to the development of a 'risk aversive' mentality in agencies and among professionals where the overriding emphasis in their work is – not to make a mistake.

Stages of change

Often in legal proceedings it is important to establish not only parents' shortcomings, and the impact on the care of their child, but whether or not there is any scope for change. Furthermore if it is felt there is scope for change, then identifying where a parent may be in that process is important. One of the best-known approaches to change is the 'Stages of Change' model, developed by Prochaska and DiClemente (1992), who were studying ways to help people to give up smoking. The model has since been applied by a variety of professionals to numerous client groups in which psychological and/or behavioural changes are required. It is often referred to in child and family proceedings by lawyers who seek to establish the scope for parental change in relation to a reasonable timescale for the child. It is used in an attempt to bring some form of measure and clarity to the complexity inherent in these cases. It appears to be used more as a measure by those acting to prevent rehabilitation and as a means of establishing how far parents are from meeting the required level of change. It is often used to support the notion that the required change cannot be achieved in the timescale for the benefit of the child. It is therefore worthy of consideration here though I have considerable doubt as to its validity in this context.

In this model they refer to six stages of change:

Stage 1 – Pre-contemplative

This is the earliest stage of change where the client is expected to present with denial perhaps claiming there are no concerns, or minimising them to a large extent. They may also be ignorant of the nature of the problems and/or the consequences.

Stage 2 – Contemplation Stage

During this stage, people become more and more aware of the potential benefits of making a change, but may feel overwhelmed at times by the challenge. This conflict creates a strong sense of ambivalence about changing. Because of this uncertainty, the contemplation stage of change can last months or even years. Many cases never make it past the contemplation phase. During this stage, you may view change as a process of giving something up as opposed to gaining any real benefits.

Stage 3 – Preparation

At this stage you may be making small changes and collecting information in preparation for more significant change. This is often considered an appropriate time for someone to see a counsellor or therapist.

Stage 4 – Action

During this stage direct action is taken toward achieving a goal. By now there is a plan but this stage can fail because the previous stages were rushed and/or are incomplete.

Stage 5 – Maintenance

The focus now is to avoid temptation and slip back into old habits. As maintenance of change is established you can become more confident and assured in the achievement.

Stage 6 – Relapse

Dealing with disappointment, frustration and a sense of failure is now the challenge. Relapse is expected and the situation can be recovered if you maintain your motivation and confidence. Analysing the reasons for the setback is important in planning the recovery.

If applying this model to smoking, alcohol problems, or substance misuse you might argue that with any behaviour change, relapses would be anticipated and a common occurrence. When you go through a relapse, you might experience feelings of failure, disappointment, and frustration. The key to success in this context is to not let these setbacks undermine your self-confidence. However, in the context of child and family law you are very fortunate to get one therapeutic opportunity aimed at change that is appropriate, timely and sensitive to the family's needs. Significant setback or failure, when it occurs, almost certainly means that there is no relapse stage or second opportunity. With this knowledge in mind there is pressure on the parents, as well as the professional providing the intervention, to succeed from the outset. With the current childcare emphasis on permanency it means there is pressure to establish stability for the child in his or her placement as early as possible; and increasingly with younger children this means adoption.

The 'stages of change' model was originally designed with smokers in mind and has been adapted quite successfully for other client groups and I feel offers a conceptual frame that is helpful. It has a simplistic, slightly formulaic approach that will be helpful to a variety of professionals in their work with clients. Its straightforward approach gives the impression that all problems can be defined in this way and therefore easily understood. Many of the families I see would be considered to be in the pre-contemplative stage. Unfortunately this would place them nowhere near the latter stages of change and in danger of being perceived as not able to change in the timescale for the child.

It is a model which does not take account of the significance of complexity, and the inevitable twists and turns in such cases. In my case study the parents were able to move relatively quickly from a pre-contemplative stage to the action and maintenance stages once a therapeutic connection had been made, suggesting the families had potential that was unrealised and untapped up to that time. It also demonstrated they were not that far from being helped toward significant change, if the contextual difficulties, including the parents' initial defensiveness, could be overcome.

The 'stages of change' model referred to here may have relevance in a general sense for the majority of individuals – though I question its validity with clients from marginalised communities in this context. Here the problems are complex, enduring and multifaceted whereby the usual rules of social convention and being relational really challenge the parents, which in turn presents a challenge for the professionals. Challenging though the context of legal proceedings may be, often taking parents to the edge may also paradoxically create a previously unforeseen (therapeutic) opportunity that if grasped, may lead to significant change.

The role of attachment

The notion of attachment suggests that a child is not seen as a passive recipient of parenting, but more that parenting occurs in an evolving relationship between parent and child. Child developmental specialists like Bruner (1986) see the various parenting factors referred to earlier as influencing child development through the notion of attachment – a key concept in understanding parent–child interaction. Bowlby (1969) proposed that an infant, baby or young child needs to develop a relationship with at least one primary caregiver – initially thought to be the mother, but now generally accepted to be whoever fulfils the caring role and is meeting the infants' needs in a sensitive, consistent and predictable fashion. Attachment is essentially the 'affectional bond' between the child and the primary caregiver. The primary caregiver's social and emotional response to the infant's need for safety, security and protection is seen as crucial and underpinning the child's developmental process. The predominant views about attachment theory and its influences have been developed originally by Bowlby, then Ainsworth (1979) and more latterly Crittenden (2005). Bowlby described three main attachment styles: secure, avoidant and insecure ambivalent/resistant. Then Ainsworth later added a fourth very important category, being that of disorganised/disorientated attachment style reflecting a lack of any coherent coping strategy in response to their caring experience. Crittenden's (2005) views have been developed in recent times to form what she terms the Dynamic Maturational Model. It differs from Bowlby's thinking in as much as it reflects Crittenden's view that attachment behaviour is a range of behavioural strategies for attracting and shaping parental behaviour in the context of a perceived threat and the need for protection.

Regardless of the definition or model most attachment theorists agree that early experiences with an attachment figure develop into an internal system of thought, sometimes called an 'internal working model' (Howe, 1995), containing memories, beliefs, expectations, emotions and behaviours about the self and others. Ideally secure attachment experience produces an empathic adult, who is secure in themselves, autonomous and interpersonally and intra-psychically balanced.

In the context of this work, I would argue attachment is very relevant from a number of perspectives. Firstly the attainment of a secure attachment experience is seen as a major protective factor for the child and therefore should be a priority in casework with families. If parents are able to achieve or potentially achieve this goal, while some aspects of parenting are still deficient, they can be seen to be doing a great deal that is beneficial for the child and themselves. Also the notion that attachment is influential throughout development and shapes personality is important from an assessment perspective. Later I will discuss assessment of parents from the point of view of the 'sense of self' and its relationship with therapeutic intervention. Therefore attachment theory is important in assessing and understanding the needs of the child as well as the parents in this work. Furthermore it informs an interactional or dynamic understanding of family relationships. Fonaghy and Target's (1997) notion of 'reflective functioning' is very pertinent here understanding as it does, interactions between parent and child in terms of the parent's ability to relate to the emotional and psychological experience of the child at any given time. This ability to 'mentalise' with or to have an 'attunement' with the child, or failure to do so, is related to a parent's self-identity and competence in the role of parent and therefore very relevant. Finally, I use attachment as a means to help frame parents' defensive reactions to professional intervention (including removal of their children) in their lives. As Dallos and Vetere (2014) put it:

> 'Attachment threat can arise when we fear rejection or abandonment, and fear that we are a disappointment to ourselves and others. This can be accompanied by deep and unprocessed feelings of shame, which if not attended to can continue to implicitly direct our defensive and self-protective strategies.'

This is a theme that runs throughout the book.

Summary of key themes

In this chapter I have tried to convey to the reader a sense of the contextual significance in these cases and in particular the influence of the 'risk aversive' professional culture. The relationship between child maltreatment, aspects of parenting, and parental breakdown, provides more than just a backdrop; it should illuminate for the reader the emotive, insecure environment and the consequent pressure it brings to both parents and professionals. I have tried to lay out the difficulties of establishing professional–client relationships in this context and how the dynamics, beginning with the first Section 47 (child protection) investigation, may affect the potential outcome. The contextual influence on client–professional relationships obviously extends beyond social workers to other professionals including Experts. The terms emanating from the Children Act 1989 such as 'significant harm' and 'good enough parenting' are referred to as socially constructed and therefore not necessarily definitive. The assessments are therefore to some extent subjective and dependent on several factors, especially relationships. Of central importance here are the references made to how psychological assessment of parents' core problems is often not attended to by social workers in favour of a 'surface-static' notion of parenting whereby they 'exhort them to change' and 'take responsibility'.

The literature on parenting provides many helpful pointers to key parameters and dimensions needed for optimum parenting, or that may be relevant to potential breakdown. However, the references also suggest there is a failure to address the multiplicity of problems faced by parents that prevents them achieving the requisite standard. Despite all the attention paid to individual parent and child factors, it is the relationship between the child and parent, and the parent with the outside world that is most important to their (child's) development. This is a key relational aspect to parents' functioning and important in many of the cases. Reference is also made to 'stages of change' commonly referred to in legal proceedings which I suggest may not always be an adequate framework, given the marginalised status of the families and case complexity.

Attachment theory is also explored in terms of its crucial influence on children's development and the enhancing qualities of 'secure attachment' in particular. The underpinning significance of attachment in this work is also reviewed in terms of its longer-term influence on parents' development and 'sense of self' in particular, as well as its role in generating parent 'defensiveness' when confronted with professionals concerns.

References

Adcock, M., White, R. and Hollows, A. (eds) (1991). *Significant Harm*. Croydon: Significant Publications.

Ainsworth, M.D.S. (1979). 'Infant-mother attachment'. *America Psychologist*, 34(10): 932–37.

Azar, S.T. and Cote, L.R. (2002). 'Sociocultural issues in the evaluation of the needs of children in custody decision making. What do our current frameworks for evaluating parenting practices have to offer?'. *International Journal of Law and Psychiatry*, 25: 193–217.

Azar, S.T. and Weinzier, R.L. (2005). 'Child maltreatment and childhood injury research: A cognitive behavioral approach'. *Journal of Pediatric Psychology*, 30(7): 598–614.

Azar, S.T., Lauretti, A.F. and Loding, B.V. (1998). 'The evaluation of parental fitness in termination of parental rights cases: A functional-contextual perspective'. *Clinical Child and Family Psychology Review*, 1(2): 77–100.

Bates, P. and Brophy, J. (1996). 'The appliance of science? The use of experts in care proceedings: A court-based study. Report of the Department of Health. London: The Stationery Office.

Belsky, J. and Vondra, J. (1989). 'Lessons from child abuse: The determinants of parenting'. In: D. Cichetti and V. Carlson (eds), *Child Maltreatment: Theory and Research on the causes and Consequences of Child Abuse and Neglect*. Cambridge: Cambridge University Press.

Bentovim, A., Barnes, G.G. and Cooklin, A. (eds) (1987). 'A family therapy approach to making decisions in child care cases'. In: A. Bentovim, G.G. Barnes and A. Cooklin (eds), *Family Therapy: Complementary Frameworks of Theory and Practice*. London: Academic Press.

Black, D., Harris Hendriks, J. and Wolkind, S. (eds) (1998). *Child Psychiatry and the Law*, 3rd edn. London: Gaskell.

Bowlby, J. (1969) *Attachment and Loss, Volume 1: Attachment*. Hogarth Press: London.

Brandon, M., Bailey, S., Belderson, P., Gardner, R., Sidebotham, P., Dodsworth, J., Warren, C. and Black, J. (2009). 'Understanding serious case reviews and their impact: A biennial analysis of serious case reviews 2005–2007'. Department for Children Schools and Families Research Report RR129.

Brophy, J., Jhutti-Johal, J. and McDonald, E. (2005). *Minority Ethnic Parents and their Solicitors and Child Protection Litigation*. Research Series 5.05. London: DCA.

Brophy, J., Jhutti-Johal, J. and Owen, C. (2003). *Significant Harm: Child Protection in a Multi-cultural Setting*. Research Series 1.03. London: DCA.

Bruner, J. (1986). *Actual Minds, Possible Worlds*. Cambridge: Harvard University Press.

Budd, K.S. (2001). 'Assessing parental competence in child protection cases: A clinical practice model'. *Clinical Child and Family Psychology Review*, 4(1): 1–18.

Budd, K.S. and Holdsworth, M.J. (1996). 'Issues in clinical assessment of minimal parenting competence'. *Journal of Clinical Child Psychology*, 25(1): 1–14.

Cann, W. (2004). 'A conceptual model for the provision of parenting support'. Paper presented at NSW Department of Community Services Research to Practice Forum, 25 November.

Children Act. (1989). London: HMSO, 1991.

Cleaver, H., Walker, S. and Meadows, P. (2004). *Assessing Children's Needs and Circumstances: The Impact of the Assessment Framework*. Jessica Kingsley: London.

Crittenden, P.M. (2005). *Using the CARE-Index for Screening, Intervention and Research*. Miami, FL: Family Relations Institute.

Dallos, R. and Vetere, A. (2014). 'Systemic therapy and attachment narratives: Attachment narrative therapy'. *Clinical Child Psychology and Psychiatry*, 19.4: 494–502.

Daniel, B. (2000). 'Judgments about parenting: What do social workers think they are doing?'. *Child Abuse Review*, 9(2): 91–107.

Dingwall, R., Eekelaar, J.M. and Murray, T. (1983). *The Protection of Children: State Intervention and Family Life*. Oxford: Blackwell.

Drummond, D.C. and Fitzpatrick, G. (2000). 'Children of substance misusing parents'. In: P. Reder, M. McClure and A. Jolley (eds), *Family Matters: Interfaces Between Child and Adult Mental Health*. London: Routledge.

Farmer, E.R.G., Sturgess, W., O'Neill, T. and Wijedasa, D. (2011). *Achieving Successful Returns from Care: What Makes Reunification Work?* London: BAAF. ISBN 978 1 907585 25 8.

Fonaghy, P. and Target, M. (1997). 'Attachment and reflective functioning. A vital role in self organisation'. *Development & Psychopathology*, 9(4): 679–700. Cambridge University Press.

Fook, J., Ryan, M. and Hawkins, L. (1997). 'Towards a theory of social work expertise'. *British Journal of Social Work*, 27(3): 399–418.

Freeman, P. and Hunt, J. (1998). *Parental Perspectives on Care Proceedings*. London: Department of Health.

Gilbert, R., Spatz Vidon, C., Browne, K., Ferguson, D., Webb, E. and Jansen, S.B. (2009). 'Burden and consequences of child maltreatment in the higher income west'. *The Lancet*, 373(9567.

Glaser, D. (1993). 'Emotional abuse'. In: C.J. Hobbs and J.M. Wynne (eds), *Clinical Pediatrics: International Practice and Research. Volume 1, Child Abuse*. London: Bailliere Tindall.

Golombok, S. (2000). *Parenting: What Really Counts?* Routledge: London.

Gopfert, M., Webster, J., Pollard, J. and Nelki, J.S. (1996). 'The assessment and prediction of parenting capacity: A community-oriented approach'. In: M. Gopfert, J. Webster and M.V. Seeman (eds), *Parental Psychiatric Disorder: Distressed Parents and their Families*. Cambridge: Cambridge University Press.

Harwin, J., Owen, M., Locke, R. and Forrester, A. (1999). Research Report – Making Care Orders Work.

Henry, L.A. and Kumar, R.C. (1999). 'Risk assessments of infants born to parents with a mental health problem or a learning disability'. In: A. Weir and A. Douglas (eds), *Child Protection & Adult Mental Health: Conflict of Interest?* Oxford: Butterworth-Heinemann.

Herbert, M. (1996). *Assessing Children in Need and Their Parents*. Leicester: BPS Books.

Hindley, N., Ramchandani, P.G. and Jones, D.P.H. (2006). 'Risk factors for recurrence of maltreatment: A systematic review'. *Archives of Disease in Childhood*, 91(9): 744–52.

Hoghughi, M. (1997). 'Parenting at the margins: Some consequences of inequality'. In: K.N. Dwivedi (ed.), *Enhancing Parenting Skills. A Guide Book for Professionals Working with Parents*. Chichester: Wiley.

Holland, S. (2009). 'Listening to children in care: A review of methodological and theoretical approaches to understanding looked after children's perspectives'. *Children and Society*, 23 (3): 226–35.

Howe, D. (1995). *Attachment Theory for Social Work Practice*. Basingstoke: Palgrave Macmillan.

Howe, D., Schofield, G., Brandon, M. and Hinings, D. (1999). *Attachment Theory and Child Maltreatment and Family Support: A Practice and Assessment Model*. Hampshire: Palgrave.

Hunt, J., MacLeod, A. and Thomas, C. (1999). *The Last Resort: Child Protection, the Courts and the 1989 Children Act*. London: The Stationery Office.

Iwaniec, D. (1995). *The Emotionally Abused and Neglected Child: Identification, Assessment and Intervention*. Chichester: Wiley.

Iwaniec, D. (2004). *Children Who Fail to Thrive: A Practice Guide*. Chichester: John Wiley & Sons.

Jacobsen, T., Miller, L.J. and Kirkwood, K. (1997). 'Assessing parenting competence in individuals with severe mental illness: A comprehensive service'. *Journal of Mental Health Administration*, 24: 189–9.

Jenuwine, M.J. and Cohler, B.J. (1999). 'Major parental psychopathology and child custody'. In: R.M. Galatzer-Levy and L. Kraus (eds), *The Scientific Basis of Child Custody Decisions*. New York: John Wiley.

Jones, D. (2001). 'The assessment of parental capacity'. In: J. Horwath (ed.), *The Child's World: Assessing Children in Need*. London: Jessica Kingsley.

Kempe, C.H., Silverman, F.N., Steele, B.F., Droegemueller, W. and Silver, H.K. (1962). 'The battered-child syndrome'. *Journal of the American Medical Association*, 181: 17–24.

Kennedy, R. (1997). 'Assessment of parenting'. *Child Abuse, Psychotherapy and the Law*. London: Free Association Books.

Maitra, B. (2003). 'Would cultural matching ensure culturally competent assessments?'. In: P. Reder, S. Duncan and C. Lucey (eds), *Studies in the Assessment of Parenting*. London: Routledge.

Masson, J.M., Pearce, J.F. and Bader K.F. (2008). 'Care profiling study'. Ministry of Justice Research Series 4.08. For Ministry of Justice and Department of Children, Schools and Families: Ministry of Justice.

Oates, M. (1984). 'Assessing fitness to parent'. In: British Agencies for Adoption and Fostering (eds), *Taking a Stand: Child Psychiatrists in Custody, Access and Disputed Adoption Cases*. London: British Agencies for Adoption and Fostering.

Parton, N., Thorpe, D. and Wattom. C. (1997). *Child Protection, Risk and Moral Order*. London: Macmillan.

Platt, D. (2008). 'Care or control? The effects of investigations and initial assessments on the social worker–parent relationship'. *Social Work Practice*, 22(3): 301–15.

Polanyi, M. (1967). *The Tacit Dimension*. New York: Anchor Books.

Prochaska, J. and DiClemente, C. (1992). 'In search of how people change: Application to addictive behaviour'. *American Psychologist*, 47(9): 1102–14.

Quinton, D. and Rutter, M. (1988). *Parenting Breakdown: The Making and Breaking of Intergenerational Links*. Aldershot: Avebury Gower.

Reder, P., Duncan, S. and Lucey, C. (2003). *Studies in the Assessment of Parenting*. London: Routledge.

Risley-Curtis, C., Stromwall, L.K., Hunt, D.T. and Teska, J. (2004). 'Identifying and reducing barriers to reunification for seriously mentally ill parents involved in child welfare cases'. *Families in Society*, 85(1): 107–19.

Roberts, J.V. (2000). 'Changing public attitudes towards corporal punishment: The effects of statutory reform in Sweden'. *Child Abuse & Neglect*, 24(8): 1027–35.

Schaffer, H.R. (1998). *Making Decisions About Children*, 2nd edn. Oxford: Blackwell.

Sheldrick, C. (1998). 'Child psychiatrists in court: Their contribution as experts in child care proceedings'. *Journal of Forensic Psychiatry*, 9(2): 249–66.

Shlonsky, A. and Wagner, D. (2005). 'The next step: Integrating actual risk assessment and clinical judgment into an evidence-based practice framework in CPS case management'. *Children and Youth Services Review*, 27: 409–27.

Sinclaire, I. (2005). *Messages from Research*. London: Jessica Kingsley.

Steinhauer, P.D. (1983). 'Assessing for parenting capacity'. *American Journal of Orthopsychiatry*, 53(3): 468–81.

Sturge, C. (1992). 'Dealing with the courts and parenting breakdown'. *Archives of Disease in Childhood*, 67(6): 745–50.

Swadi, H. (1994). 'Parenting capacity and substance misuse: An assessment scheme'. *ACPP Review & Newsletter*, 16(5): 237–44.

Teti, D.M. and Candelaria, M.A. (2002). 'Parenting competence'. In: M.H. Bornstein (ed.), *Handbook of Parenting*, 2nd edn. Volume 4: *Social Conditions and Applied Parenting* (pp. 149–80). New Jersey: Lawrence Erlbaum.

Thoburn, J. (with Making Research Count Consortium) (2009). 'Effective interventions for complex families where there are concerns about or evidence of a child suffering significant harm'. London Centre for Excellence and Outcomes in Children and Young People's Services (C4EO).

Tufnell, G., Cottrell, D. and Geogiades, D. (1996). '"Good practice" for expert witnesses'. *Clinical Child Psychology & Psychiatry*, 1: 365–83.

Turney, D., Platt, D., Selwyn, J. and Farmer, E. (2011). *Government Research – Social Work Assessment of Children in Need: What Do We Know? Messages From Research*. Bristol: University of Bristol.

Wade, J., Biehal, N., Farrelly, N. and Sinclair, I. (2010). *Outcomes for Children Looked After for Reasons of Abuse or Neglect: The Consequences of Staying in Care or Returning Home*. London: Department for Education.

Wolkind, S. (1994). 'Legal aspects of child care'. In: M. Rutter, E. Taylor and L. Hersov (eds), *Child and Adolescent Psychiatry: Modern Approaches*, 3rd edn. Oxford: Blackwell.

Woodcock, J. (2003). 'The social work assessment of parenting: An exploration'. *British Journal of Social Work*, 33(1): 87–106.

Chapter 3

Research questions, method and emerging themes

A reflexive journey

Aims

The aims of the study are encapsulated in the following research questions that have emerged via my experience in the field, collaboration with peers, and consultation with leading Experts:

- How can professionals involved in legal proceedings be helped to identify families with therapeutic potential?
- What are the critical aspects of therapy in this context?
- Can the data obtained in this study be harnessed to provide the basis of a framework that would guide professional activity (identify families) and be predictive of outcome?

Rationale

The above research questions meant that I was going to obtain data that was individualistic and relational, capturing experiential insights and emotional reaction. With this in mind I used a mixed qualitative method (Heuristic inquiry; Case Study) approach that best captured and appreciated different types of data of this kind. As a process, I expected to make what I knew implicitly – via my extensive casework experience in this field, to become more explicit. My intention was to reveal what knowledge, frames of reference, tacit understanding, skills and other factors are influential in therapeutic work.

The inquiry would help illuminate data specific to this context particularly that which affects the activity of professionals as well as the behaviour of parents. It was also important to understand the potential impact on key relationships the parents had with the professionals involved in the case. I hoped to reveal critical aspects of therapeutic assessment and intervention in this context, which apart from being influential for therapists and Experts, may also guide wider professional activity, and signpost those families who may benefit from appropriate and timely intervention or assessment. Much of my early experience as an Expert in this context was a steep learning curve. As my experience grew it accumulated implicitly-based knowledge, intuitive skills, and tacit frames of reference that were specific for this context. I was aware I had also utilised experience from my work in other contexts – albeit modified to support my endeavour in this work. This, combined with what I have drawn from the literature, enabled me to build some expertise. This was partially known and felt by me, increasingly recognised by others, but needed to be more explicit and understood. The intention was to reveal this so that it could potentially contribute to the emerging framework.

The potential obstacles, the twists and turns that occur in a study of this nature, are rarely completely predictable from the outset and naturally require some adjustment with the benefit of the unfolding experience. I support the view of Aguinaldo (2004) who said that 'qualitative researchers should not be constrained within a methodological straightjacket and must be allowed to utilise whatever methods necessary to explore the phenomenon under consideration'. He does, however, make the point that it is not just the choices, but the reasons for those choices, and the researcher's theoretical interests secured by those choices, that need to be made explicit and held up to scrutiny. I hope I have done that.

Method

The study utilised a combination of Heuristic and Case Study (augmented with Narrative analysis) design methods. The five case studies are presented in greater detail in the next chapter. The heuristic inquiry took as its focus the author's experience of several hundred cases where therapeutic assessment and intervention had taken place in childcare legal proceedings over a period of ten years. Quantitative methodology was not considered even though there were large numbers of cases. Unfortunately the casework was undertaken without any planning to systematically obtain quantitative data at a later stage.

Moustakas (1990) describes heuristic research as:

> an organised and systematic form for investigating human experience. From the beginning and throughout an investigation, heuristic research involves self-search, self-dialogue, and self-discovery; the research question and the methodology flow out of inner awareness, meaning, and inspiration.

This method requires the researcher to have had a:

> direct, personal encounter with the phenomenon being investigated and undergone the experience in a vital, intense and full way. It demands the total presence, honesty, maturity, and integrity of a researcher, who not only strongly desires to know and understand, but is willing to commit endless hours of sustained immersion and focused concentration on one central question.

The heuristic inquiry used three independent Experts to drill down deep into the author's experience of this work in order to make more explicit what had already become implicitly known (e.g. tacit knowledge, frameworks). Each of the Experts brought their own particular expertise to the interviews which were audiotaped and later transcribed to ascertain emerging themes.

Case Study sample

The Case Study sample was made up of five from seven families whom I had previously assessed as suitable for therapy in legal proceedings, who engaged in the process with me, and were eventually successfully reunited as a family. I did not know when I contacted the families again if they were still together; so identified seven families hoping to get a minimum of five who would participate. To fit the criteria the sample families needed to have remained together as a family and not currently involved in legal proceedings or a section 47 (child protection) investigation. I identified my sample by retrospectively selecting the last seven cases from my case records that met the criteria referred to above.

The families ranged from a time period of one to four years since my last session with them. During the course of my work with the families I had already informed them of the research project and of their potential involvement one day – should they agree to participate. The parents invariably remembered that conversation when I contacted them again to discuss their involvement. The parents were offered the opportunity to become involved in the study and five of the seven families agreed to participate. The two who did not participate were still together and met the criteria but declined because of the influence of life events at that time. One family had just had a baby; the other had recently lost an application to revoke a care order on the child in question. The child was still with them and the agencies very happy with their care. The court was sympathetic to their application but felt revocation of the care order was premature at this stage. The case had been in court for many months and they were emotionally exhausted and naturally disappointed and wanted time to recover.

First stage of the case study review

Prior to reviewing the above cases and as part of my mental preparation for this exercise I randomly selected a case where a family was successfully rehabilitated and reviewed my analysis, recommendations and the eventual outcome to see what thoughts, ideas it stirred within me with the passing of several years. Reviewing the data again I felt my 'emerging framework' to be relevant and had I been more consciously aware, may have guided my work with the family more effectively at the time. I was curious to compare my longer-term reflections with theirs and seeing them again generated excitement as well as some trepidation. Their longer-term reflections would be invaluable to the emerging framework. I anticipated they would be able speak more openly and authoritatively now that they were comfortably beyond that time of assessments, constant observation and scrutiny.

It was self-evident that the parents had made significant improvements – usually across a number of domains – in order to win through legal proceedings and secure the return of their children. There were in each case therapeutic issues that were addressed as well as other key factors that were influential as far as the courts were concerned. In each of the cases, despite a problematic history of working with professionals, there was evidence of significant improvement in this area even before the families were finally reunited. This had required a huge turnaround on the part of the parents who will have had to address significant issues of central importance to the court – including acknowledging their culpability and responsibility for events leading up to the removal of the children to foster care. They will have had to address criticisms of their previous care as well as attachment difficulties anticipated with the return of their child after a significant separation.

I wanted to obtain from the parents their reflections on the critical events leading to the removal of the child and their perception of that now; whether the new, longer-term reflection had provided new insight or greater understanding that had influenced their approach to the care of their children now. Similarly I wanted to establish if the significant changes in family functioning had been maintained over this time and been reflected in other areas; for example, were they still together as a family unit and functioning quite well? Were they able to deal with professionals more effectively? In three of the five cases reviewed and followed up there had been domestic violence and alongside this, four cases where serious substance/alcohol misuse occurred. Where domestic violence and alcohol/substance misuse occur together the consequences are often very serious for the children's well-being (Farmer *et al.*, 2011; Parton *et al.*, 1997). I was interested to know how they had responded to the long-term challenges.

While I was able to see turning points in the process of each case, I now wanted to obtain the parents' perception of those events and what part the therapeutic intervention had played. I wanted their perceptions even though their feedback potentially laid bare the effectiveness (or otherwise) of my role. Again this would influence the emerging framework.

Preparation for the case study interviews

I had developed questions that would be common to each case as well as case-specific questions. Although I intended there to be structure and to be guided by the questions I wanted the interviews to be conversational so that ideas could potentially develop. In its simplest form I was looking for their ideas of how they were helped, how they helped themselves, and how others in similar predicaments might benefit from their experience. This process would be more than just a question and answer session, with each of us developing and enriching the process with memories, reflections and potentially new ideas. In this I was to some extent influenced by Fontana and Frey (2000) who say 'forget about the how to do rules and adapt to ever changing situations you may face'. The purpose of the semi-structured interview schedule was to provide sufficient structure and focus without inhibiting meaningful conversation and potential creativity. With this in mind the basis of a semi-structured interview was developed.

Semi-structured interview

Each of the sample cases agreed to participate in a semi-structured interview (SSI). The interview invariably began before the first SSI question was asked and quickly developed a life of its own. The SSI therefore did not provide a formal structure for the interview, but more of a guide and reference point ensuring key areas relating to the research questions were covered. The guiding questions I had identified were:

1. Did they remember our first meeting? – We compared experiences, expectations and what information we had received about each other.
2. How did we arrive at an understanding and then a plan?
3. At what point did parents feel they had turned a corner?
4. How did relationships with professionals improve; when and why?
5. What was my part (with other professionals) in this?
6. Did they change on the inside and/or outside?
7. What would they say (with the benefit of experience) to the parent they were then – if they met them now? This was sometimes reframed as: what advice would you give to parents in a similar position to you then, if you met them now?
8. What were the good aspects of a very difficult experience, or what or who was helpful?
9. How has it left them feeling now in terms of:-

   Reflections on the experience;
   Relationship with partner and child;
   Relationships with professionals;
   Sense of culpability and regret.

10. How did they see the future?

Although the questions are listed in an order 1 to 10, it never proceeded in that way. We often arrived at a question more as the conversation unfolded and/or it felt like the right time to ask it. Sometimes the issues that questions were meant to provoke had already been dealt with as the discussion (rather than question and answer) naturally unfolded. The parents had a story to tell again and that developed a life of its own. I also told them my longer-term reflections of their case as part of the discussion. Despite resurrecting intense feelings in relation to difficult experiences, the process felt natural, shared and safe. The questions were as necessary for my mental preparation for the SSI as they were for providing some structure and a guiding influence in the interviews themselves. In most of the interviews I rarely looked at the questions except at the beginning and the end, making sure all the issues had been addressed. By the end I felt as if we had been through an experience together again and the process of recollection, and telling it once again, was of mutual benefit.

Analysis of findings

According to Moustakas (1996) heuristic research is defined as 'a process of internal search through which one discovers the nature and meaning of experience and develops methods and procedures for investigation and analysis'. Therefore analysis of data is an ongoing and integral part of the process and not restricted to the final phase of the study as in other methods.

The data obtained from the case study (assessment and therapeutic reports) and then shared with parents in a co-constructive fashion were analysed with a view to emerging themes and patterns that relate to the research questions. This process was enhanced by using a narrative analysis approach which was particularly helpful in revealing aspects of the parents' self-identity – a central theme in the 'emerging framework'. This process involved an analysis of the copious notes resulting from the transcription process which were then organised and grouped according to emerging themes. This process captured the parents' longer-term reflections as it related to therapeutic work, professional activity and indications for an emerging framework. To assist with this process, control for bias and increase authenticity, the emerging data is reviewed at each stage with 'critical friends'. The meaning extrapolated from the data will have undergone a rigorous process involving: my own re-visiting of the original material; then reviewing with parents in a semi-structured interview; and reviewing the data and analysis with 'critical friends' and interested peers who collaborated with this process.

As the data from each method was analysed and became more coherent, its relationship with the developing framework began to emerge. To enhance this process I met with other Experts, agencies and relevant professionals who have extensive experience of this work to share my findings and receive critical feedback.

The challenge was then to harness the meaningful data from the study with the other significant influences to form the basis of a coherent, usable, working framework.

Case study data – emerging themes and analysis

All the case study semi-structured interviews were audiotaped and later transcribed. This is a very detailed, painstaking process which involved taking copious amounts of notes to determine categories and groupings which eventually become organised and then refined. After listening to the interview recordings and reading and re-reading the transcriptions, several clear themes emerged from the data. The groupings I finally settled with were naturally influenced by the research questions that were very much in my mind throughout this process. The emerging themes were:

- Context and professional activity;
- Aspects relevant to therapy; and
- Parental change.

The process of exploring the case study data was enhanced by the use of narrative analysis. This illuminated relevant aspects of the parents' self-identity. This has proved to be a useful qualitative methodology where the numbers of participants are small, and where the focus of inquiry is upon the relationship between the 'self' and culture (Weatherhead, 2011). Burck (2005) has explored this from the perspective of the 'systemic researcher'. She refers to three levels of self-construction that I have adapted for use here. These are: accounts, reflections and positioning, with sub-levels beyond this depending on the detail and nature of your inquiry. The levels are illuminated by posing the core question: What are the effects of all this (participant's narratives) on the participant's self-construct (Weatherhead, 2011)? This is represented diagrammatically in Figure 3.1.

Context and professional activity

All of the parents talked very positively about their lawyers who – more than most other professionals – could relate to their distress at that time. Having met their lawyers some of whom were responsible for commissioning me in the first place, I can confirm they cared a great deal and believed in their clients' (often undefined) potential. This relationship in all five cases was felt by them to be profound and sustained them through the darkest times and kept alive the 'hope' (Flaskas, 1997). The lawyers were referred to by the families in a way you might have expected them to refer to their social worker, therapist or some other member of the caring professions. The lawyers were probably more accepting of them than other professionals at that time and were clearly, because of their role, on their side. This allowed the parent to 'engage' with them at a more productive level and have the kind of necessary dialogue they were often unable to have with other professionals. It was clear to me in all five cases that the lawyers were motivated to help and believed in their clients' credibility – it was not simply just doing their job.

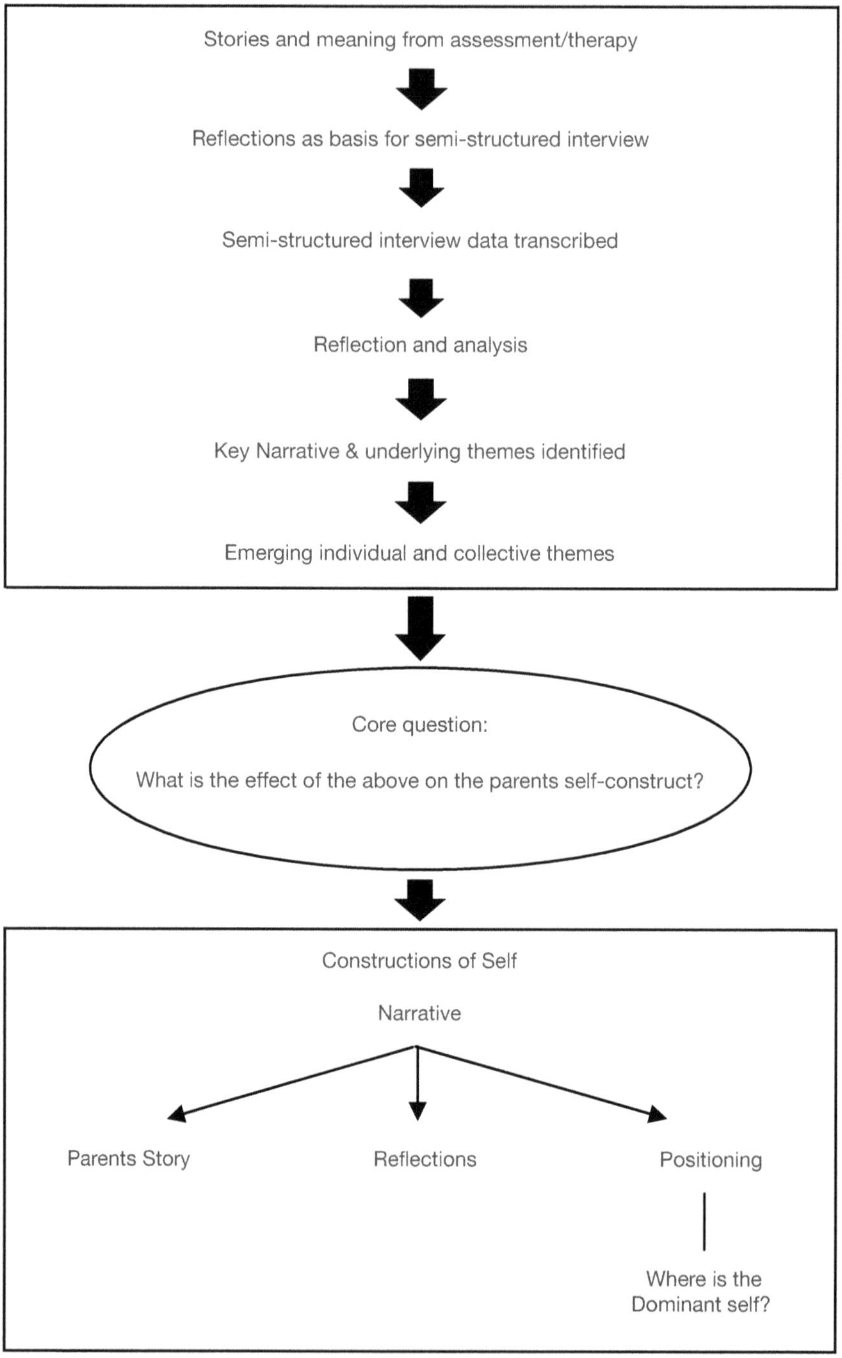

Figure 3.1 Identification and process of parents' narratives

Some parents experienced a real turning point when they felt the Judge began to connect with them and their predicament – especially if it was something disputed with the professionals or specific to the child, such as favouring increased contact with their child. Finding the capacity to trust anyone, especially professionals, was fundamental for them. They now felt the competence of professionals, alongside a decision to trust them or not, was something to be assessed by them, and not assumed or taken as a given. For example, sharing sensitive information with a professional was now approached with caution, feeling it may be used against them at a later stage.

Often, because of the unstable professional context of childcare social work the parents would have experienced several if not many changes of worker. This also occurred with children's guardians. Sometimes this would happen at critical times and they would be left without a social worker and/or guardian for an extended period. Establishing a good working relationship with professionals was very problematic in this relatively unstable professional environment. This was critical for the families who needed welfare support, as well as help with other essential matters, such as contact arrangements with the child, that needed to be organised during this time. Even where a trusting relationship existed with an individual social worker the parents now seemed more aware of the power of agencies to make key decisions.

These families had experienced the power of agencies like the Child and Family Court Advisory and Support Service (CAFCASS), Social Services and the Courts and knew that they could override any decision made at the parent–social worker level. Many parents also felt that by opening up to social workers and children's guardians that they were providing them with potential evidence rather than laying the basis for 'working together'. There is a serious dichotomy here between making a relationship with a social worker and cooperating with the professional process and obtaining the help you need, while avoiding providing evidence that will potentially lose you the case. The social worker too is in an invidious position; are they building a case against the parents, or are they helping and supporting them? (Woodcock, 2003) Juggling both roles is a real challenge for the social worker (Parton *et al.*, 1997). The process of gaining evidence in this way directly militates against the development of a working/trusting relationship with parents.

The parents were also aware of the manner in which I give my evidence – either in the form of a report and/or via cross-examination. This is a very tricky area that I address not only early on but throughout my involvement in the case. I say to parents that before I submit a report we will discuss my findings, recommendations, etc., so there are 'no surprises there for them'. While I am as open as I can be, the context of legal proceedings is undoubtedly a significant obstacle in building any kind of working (including therapeutic) relationship with parents. The child protection (statutory) social work role brings with it cultural as well as agency pressures. While I do not have the same pressures, any professional, including Experts, can easily be absorbed into the culture and associated mindset, and by doing so sub-consciously accept the local authority account of events as facts, rather than perceptions or, to some extent at least, debatable narratives. The danger here for Experts is that they arrive to undertake an assessment having already (subconsciously) largely formed a view of the case – something which they may inadvertently convey to the parents when they meet them. Related to this is the position taken by Experts in relation to the family and the extent to which they are prepared to try and engage them (Davies, 2009).

The parents largely acknowledged culpability and responsibility for the events that led up to the removal of the children. However, there were important caveats from their point of view. With the benefit and freedom of long-term hindsight they were able to describe serious shortcomings in the system as well as raise concerns about professional competence, and in one case this was supported by the Judge. There was significant conflict between the parents and the social worker in three of the cases; when the social worker was changed there was an immediate improvement in relations and very positive feedback about them from the parents.

What came over strongly was a sense of parental disempowerment and at times a fear of professionals. The parents' reaction was often judged by professionals to be 'resistance' on the part of the parents, or evidence of their inability to 'work with the department'. Examination of social work assessments as well as research by Woodcock (2003) suggests social workers in this context tend not to take into account or address 'underlying psychological problems', the lack of which results in unrealistic expectations and potentially inaccurate assessments of them. This may contribute to their inability to relate to the context-specific nature of the parents' overall experience resulting in: the parents being defined as resistant, 'aggressive', 'unable to work with the department'; or worst of all when frustration boils over, such as displaying anger management problems.

Parents perceived professionals as often not understanding their predicament especially relating to their experience of losing their children to care (see Table 3.1). The parents were highly stressed often with secondary symptoms of depression and anxiety. Rather than the stress being understood in terms of the context, they felt it was at times turned against them, almost confirming them as incompetent parents who were unable to cope.

Even when the situation improved for parents they still felt disempowered, as if most of the professionals were against them. It seemed to me many parents often felt culturally alienated and therefore living in another world from the professionals, and struggled to relate to them.

Aspects of therapeutic work

Often the parents found it difficult to articulate what the therapy was, though they were able to describe meaningful aspects for them, some of which are quoted here: 'being listened to'; 'not being judged'; 'feeling someone was on my side'; 'someone was prepared to believe me'; 'you seemed to understand'; 'you knew what you were talking about'; 'I remembered the way you talked about other cases, I felt you must know a lot'. In many respects, the therapeutic qualities referred to by parents you would expect most therapists would be able to bring to the situation. They also refer to what I have described as being 'therapeutic' in approach, whatever the role. This is taking a position of understanding, sensitivity and caring, and listening in relation to the parents and their circumstances.

While accruing a great deal of specialist experience in this field I have also worked with refugees, and other very marginalised groups. In contexts such as these where you might expect more than the usual communication problems, the use of language, and (therapist) flexibility and creativity are likely to be important elements (Papadopoulos, 2002). These were also contexts where I became familiar with working in a variety of environments outside the clinic/therapy room setting to make therapeutic work more accessible, but also meaningful to these clients. I acknowledge here my own motivation to help marginalised groups, which has its empathic roots, at least in part, located deep in my past.

It is also evident that some of the therapeutic skills – not exclusive to psychotherapy – such as being non-judgemental, sensitive and an empathic listener, are relevant for other professionals in this work. It seems that the parents' lawyers in this study were able to employ these skills with success. The data here also indicates that it is not simply a question of having the skill set – but being able to work in a way that is not constrained by the context (Cecchin, 1987) and whereby you can draw on aspects of 'self' to make the therapy relevant.

Relational factors were crucial to the whole process. If 'early work and engagement' was successful it often led to a context whereby parental reflection became possible. As the relationship unfolded it became easier to examine their narrative, perceptions and underlying emotions, without fear of prejudice (Bugental *et al.*, 2002). Parents valued professionals who were less formal with them; who could 'temporarily step outside the role' or 'put something of self on offer' in order to help create a more relational context. However, the sub-text for the parents throughout this was – 'how can we get the children back?' and provided the basis of their motivation. Where it was appropriate I shared with them my experience of other similar cases that had been successful without compromising confidentiality. Farmer, *et al.* (2011) identified this kind of motivation in parents as a positive indicator in the reunification of families. This therapeutic strategy took the focus outside of themselves for a while so that highly sensitive issues could be explored with less intensity. The parents related well to hearing the experience of other families I used as examples – what I refer to as 'parallel cases'. They also appeared to benefit from knowing other families had the same or similar problems and had faced similar challenges.

It did not mean the solutions would necessarily be the same for them but that there was a potential route to reunification, one already travelled by others to whom they could relate.

Woodcock (2003) refers to the importance of understanding the underlying emotional and psychological issues that could potentially explain parents' motivation, behaviour, and ability to relate at so many levels. The two cases of single mothers Jean (Case Study 5) and Sheila (Case Study 4) had previously had problems of domestic violence with unsuitable, sometimes dangerous partners. The therapeutic approach in these cases was enabling the mothers to develop a 'sense of relationship', as I described it in many of the reports. These were young mothers who had experienced severe disruption, abuse and trauma in their backgrounds and had been unable to develop a very mature sense of relationship. For example, in a matter of days they could go from meeting someone, becoming intimate, trusting them at various levels, and making longer-term commitments (partner becoming step-father) involving their children. These relationships developed at such pace leaving a great deal to chance especially the safety of the mother or the children and having no solid relationship (let alone parental) base. The children would have to adjust to a new partner/step-parents coming and going with all its associated dynamics and instability. In the Knight family (Case Study 4) it had a profound effect on the children's well-being, leading to their removal.

The therapy helped Sheila realise a concept of relationships that was defined in developmental terms; she was able to refer to her relationships as 'teenage-like' and to herself as needing to grow up. In this approach the history for this kind of relationship behaviour alongside tolerating partner abuse is explored. Understanding and relating the needs of the children was key. Any partner relationship had to be considered in these terms which often required the parents to be more 'attuned' to the needs of their children.

Sheila and Jean needed help with aspects of their sense of self; issues such as self-worth became significant especially as they related their expectations of a partner, and his role/relationship with the children in which their safety and well-being was paramount.

Four dimensions of therapeutic work emerged as relevant in this context:

1 Doing stuff; refers to psycho-educational approaches, such as 'anger management', relationship work, aspects of parenting and anxiety management (see Table 3.2)
2 Becoming reflective, and narrative work
3 Me and you (therapeutic relationship)
4 Professional context; acting as a (therapeutic) link between and within the often separate worlds of the professional system and the family.

It also became clear how the work with the parents benefitted from moving fluidly between the dimensions according to the parents' needs. It involved therapeutic work with the wider family/professional system as well as within the family itself at differing levels. The work sometimes involved an educative function and sometimes required a consultative role to be taken with the parents and/or the professionals. All of this potential activity is of course predicated on the success or otherwise of 'early work and engagement'.

In each of the five case studies referred to earlier and in many other examples within my experience, the therapeutic work invariably ended abruptly and prematurely – often as or just prior to reunification. This was openly acknowledged by Social Services as a financially driven decision and not based on the family's ongoing need to consolidate and/or maintain progress. In some cases Social Services dramatically changed their position of resisting reunification in a case to accepting it almost overnight and putting families back together in haste and without appropriate support and contingencies.

This of course fails to prepare families adequately and as a consequence, reunification fails in such a way it incurs further distress and damage for the children, often eliminating the chance of any further attempts at a later stage.

The experience of losing children to care and then the subsequent battle in legal proceedings to have them reunified was a profound experience for the parents. They each frequently re-experienced feelings associated with events, such as the removal of their child or being in court. The Smith parents (Case Study 1) in particular talked of going to bed at night and waking up in the morning with the same feeling of stress they experienced during the worst of their ordeal. 'It's the last thing you think of at night – the first thing you think of in the morning when you wake'. They described the feelings as being intense, though relatively brief, before their conscious mind is awakened to the realisation that those circumstances do not now exist – that the children are at home with them.

In three of the case study examples they could not imagine a time when the experience would not be profound for them and re-experienced in this way. It was reminiscent of the 'malignant memories' (Pynoos and Nader, 1993) I had encountered in my work with refugee families. Like refugee families they felt most other people could not understand or relate to this experience. They all felt that most of the professionals did not relate to their (parental) experiences of losing their children to foster care in this way, appearing to them to be detached and unconcerned.

Each of the parents indicated to me that I conveyed concern for them, appeared to care, and related to their experience without prejudice. Although it took longer in some cases than others to establish the necessary trust they all felt I was perceived to be on their side – even though I again denied I was taking sides – it was their (necessary) perception. With my involvement they felt there was 'hope' which developed as a central feature in each case. They felt I could act as a bridge between them and the professionals they were in conflict with, perceiving this very positively – even though it often did not result in the change they desired. In the conversational nature of it all I was able to remind them of uncomfortable times when they could have easily rejected me as they had other professionals. This kind of frankness felt comfortable and helped dig deeper into the experience.

We recalled how we had been able to maintain a dialogue throughout, whatever the tension or potential conflict. Some parents referred to me not 'judging' them and 'listening to their side of the story'. I also came over as having sympathy for their predicament. We also recalled some 'straight talking' or 'being honest' that took place at critical times. What was interesting was that some parents engaged almost at the outset as if intuitively they felt they could trust me. The same parents had something I could not easily quantify at that time, but I knew I could work with them and they had some, as yet, undefined potential that was worthy of further exploration. I felt this early on with some families while with others it took longer and the process was more cautious and incremental; but nevertheless I felt a sense of a process being underway. Unfortunately, in many other families this of course was not the case.

I was now able to identify those parents I considered had 'some chance' compared to others where it was more of a struggle, feeling stuck with no sense of a process underway. I was able to pinpoint the various levels of therapeutic potential and the influential factors that would contribute to a working framework. Important in this was understanding parental differences in terms of their characteristics, the significant contextual and other influential factors, and where this might place them on a continuum of therapeutic chance. This was a continuum whereby parents could be perceived as having defining (relational) characteristics with potential movement either way, dependent on a variety of factors including therapeutic and other interventions. Unfortunately in many cases the problems are overwhelming and it is far too late in the process to help them in this way. The continuum I am proposing would have gradations and define the whole range of parents who find their way to legal proceedings and being perceived on the basis of the assessment criteria as having either: 'no chance', 'some chance', or 'every chance' of engaging with therapeutic intervention and being rehabilitated with their children.

Parental perception of change

The parents reported several significant changes during the period of assessment and therapeutic involvement with me. Firstly, there grew an acknowledgement of their culpability as well as responsibility for their actions that led to the children being placed in foster care. They frequently still held criticism of some of the professionals and the perceived unfairness of the system– but it was now balanced and set against an acceptance of their role and responsibility in the key events that transpired.

During therapy, the process of reflection had allowed them to critically uncover a self-perception that was often full of contradiction. For example the father in the Morris family (Case Study 2) at one stage saw himself as: a serious substance abuser, having a violent relationship with his wife, a self-confessed adolescent, and being a caring parent of four children. Here there was no dominant self-identity as it seemed each (determined by context) competed for preference. There were inherent contradictions in these competing self-identities; while he and his wife could, with some difficulty, adjust to them in their relationship, this resulted in a chaotic lifestyle, disruption and even trauma for the children, and a range of other very serious family problems.

The self-identity issues sometimes resulted in a hardening of their position with agencies, thus compounding the problems and eventually leading to the children's placement in care. Again in the Morris case, the father, when relating to agencies, adopted a dominant notion of self, which was angry and defensive, especially early on in the process. Examples of this narrative are: 'they are fools; there is nothing they can do anyway'. Later he recognised how he had been arrogant and 'underestimated the power of the agencies involved'.

There was also a positioning in respect of his relationship with his wife that he eventually defined as 'teenager-like', and potentially aggressive – not seeing the true extent of the wider implications for their relationship, especially the impact on the children. His identity as a husband or partner was seemingly separate from that of being a parent – as if the one was unconnected and did not impact on the other. The therapy allowed reflection on competing aspects of self-identity and the resulting positioning that had taken place.

In his words – 'I can't keep living like a teenager, I have to grow up sometime' – he was able to reflect on the contradictions and conflicts in his various self-identities, and the way that led to a positioning, either in relation to disputes with his wife, or conflict with professionals or even society in general. He was able to recognise that serious substance misuse, domestic violence and a chaotic lifestyle are not congruent with the kind of parenting his children needed. He also eventually recognised that whatever the agencies' views of his behaviour he did not want this lifestyle for his children. Within this he was able to acknowledge his culpability for what had happened as well as responsibility for what he/they could change. This was now seen as separate from the criticism he levelled at professionals and the system. He had previously blamed them for nearly everything and that defensiveness affected his positioning in relation to them. There was room for both in his understanding now, rather than one obfuscating the other. This kind of therapeutic work is what Dallos and Vetere (2008) refer to as 'Attachment Narrative Therapy' where creating a secure base, exploring narrative and attachments, and considering alternatives are important elements.

Findings from both of the research methods have referred to the importance of the professional context and how this affects the nature of the work of all professionals, including Experts, as well as the defensiveness of parents. A lot of reference has been made to therapist qualities and to what extent it is influential in 'early work and engagement' – not only for a meaningful

Table 3.1 Psycho-educational involvement

	Psycho-education	*Anger management*	*Sense of relationship work*	*Aspects of parenting*	*Attachment issue*
Case 1	✓			✓	✓
Case 2	✓			✓	✓
Case 3	✓	✓		✓	✓
Case 4	✓		✓	✓	✓
Case 5	✓	✓	✓	✓	✓

Table 3.2 Parent – Professional relationships

	Good relationship lawyer	*Good relationship social worker – beginning*	*Good relationship social worker – end*	*Encouraged to separate*
Case 1	√		√	√
Case 2	√		√	√
Case 3	√		√	√
Case 4	√		√	Single parent
Case 5	√		√	Single parent

assessment, but also therapy work, should that be possible. The heuristic interviews in particular, identified various interactional phenomena and means of being communicative such as 'present moment' or 'open moments' where the usual defences can be by-passed, opening up relational possibilities. We considered how being 'therapeutic' has potential for all professionals working in this context. Working in such challenging circumstances, the data points to the therapist (and other professionals) being able to (comfortably) 'step outside the role', temporarily at times, in order to put on show aspects of self and empathically relate.

I have also made reference to moving fluidly between therapeutic dimensions according to parents' needs at the time and maintaining momentum. 'Openness' that potentially relates to parents' sense of 'hope' was identified as a therapeutic quality that seemed to underpin much of the work. From both the case study and heuristic interviews emerged qualities relating to the therapist, as well as the parents, that increased chances of a successful outcome.

The case study data benefitted from narrative analysis and focused on the critical self-identity issues (Burck, 2005) of the parents. Identifying aspects of self-identity, and in particular significant and competing contradictions among their various self-identities, revealed significant changes for parents both internally and externally during the course of therapy.

Identifying aspects of parents' self and their relational ability was related to whether they had 'no chance, some chance or every chance' of benefitting from therapeutic intervention. This, as with most of the rest of the data was relevant to the emerging framework.

References

Aguinaldo, J.P. (2004). 'Rethinking validity in qualitative research from a social constructionist', *The Qualitative Report*, 9(1): 127–36, March.

Bugental, J., Schneider, K.J. and Pierson, J.F. (2002). *The Handbook of Humanistic Psychology: Leading Edges in Theory, Research and Practice*. London: SAGE.

Burck, C. (2005). 'Comparing qualitative research methodologies for systemic research: The use of grounded theory, discourse analysis and narrative analysis'. *Journal of Family Therapy*, 27(3): 237–62.

Cecchin, G. (1987). 'Hypothesizing, circularity and neutrality revisited: An invitation to curiosity'. *Family Process*, 26(4): 405–13.

Dallos, R. and Vetere, A. (2008). 'Systemic therapy and attachment narratives'. *Journal of Family Therapy*, 30(4): 374–85.

Davies, M. (2009). 'Families on the edge: Therapy in the context of child care legal proceedings'. *The Psychotherapist*, Issue 41, Spring.

Farmer, E.R.G., Sturgess, W., O'Neill, T. and Wijedasa, D. (2011). *Achieving Successful Returns from Care: What Makes Reunification Work?* London: BAAF. ISBN 978 1 907585 25 8.

Flaskas, C. (1997). 'Engagement and the therapeutic relationship in systemic therapy'. *Journal of Family Therapy*, 19(3): 263–82.

Fontana, A. and Frey, J.H. (2000). 'The interview: From structured questions to negotiated text'. In: N.K. Denzin and Y.S. Lincoln (eds), *Handbook of Qualitative Research*. 2nd edn. Thousand Oaks, CA: SAGE Publications.

Moustakas, C. (1996). *Being In, Being For, Being With*. Northvale, NJ: Jason Atonson

Moustakas, C. (1990). *Heuristic Research*. London: SAGE.

Papadopoulos, R.K. (2002.) *Therapeutic Care for Refugees: No Place Like Home*. London: Karnac.

Parton, N., Thorpe, D. and Wattom. C. (1997). *Child Protection, Risk and Moral Order*. London: Macmillan.

Pynoos, R. and Nader, K. (1993). 'Issues in the treatment of post-traumatic stress in children and adolescents'. In: J.P. Wilson and B. Raphael (eds), *International Handbook of Traumatic Stress Syndromes* (pp. 535–49). New York: Plenum.

Weatherhead, S. (2011). 'Narrative analysis: An often overlooked approach'. *Clinical Psychology Forum* 218, February, pp. 47–52.

Woodcock, J. (2003). 'The social work assessment of parenting: An exploration'. *British Journal of Social Work*, 33(1): 87–106.

Part II

Families on the edge

Chapter 4

Five case studies

Examples of engagement in therapy and successful rehabilitation

CASE 1 – The Smith Family

Case background and professional concerns

This case involves a family with five children aged between four years and 13 years. The mother has been married previously but her first husband died tragically in a motorcycle accident. Neither parent had children from a previous relationship.

The Social Services had become involved with the family following referrals of domestic violence that had been taking place for some time prior to the removal of the children to foster care. The mother also had a history of depression and periodic alcohol misuse and had been generally resistant to professional intervention. Prior to my involvement, previous assessments that had been undertaken had indicated the episodes of domestic violence were related to the mother's episodic depression and alcohol problem. After several incidents

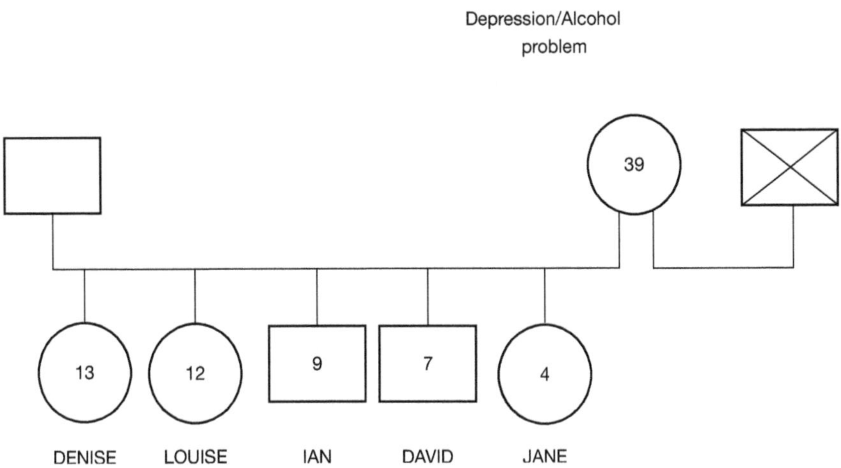

Figure 4.1 Case 1 – The Smith Family

of reported domestic violence and then the mother being found drunk in charge of the children, the children were removed in an emergency to foster placements following which care proceedings were commenced. The two youngest children, Jane and David were initially placed together, but for most of their time in foster care the children were in separate placements. The parents had significant marital problems and the father was known to have had several affairs that contributed significantly to the tension in their relationship. Alongside the concerns for the children's well-being, the parents, the mother in particular, were perceived to be at best intolerant and frequently hostile by most professionals. The father felt equally frustrated with the professionals and resistant to their intervention, but (despite his feelings) was able to relate better with them. The mother was at best intolerant, frequently challenging and sometimes angry toward them. She had been assessed by the clinical psychologist who preceded my involvement as having an IQ of 145 and was clearly very intelligent. She was prone to debate everything in detail and wherever possible 'win the argument' with professionals. The combination of the concerns the Social Services had for the children and the mother's perceived hostility toward them was in particular preventing any meaningful dialogue from taking place between them. Following the removal of the children almost any communication or attempted dialogue between the Social Services and the parents resulted in further conflict which inevitably led to legal proceedings.

Summary of the sessions

I first met the mother at the Court having already undertaken an assessment of the case documents only (often referred to as a 'paper assessment'). I was attending the court expecting to be cross-examined on my assessment when, during a hiatus in proceedings, the Judge suggested that I meet with the mother while we were at court and establish whether it was possible to engage her in a therapeutic assessment. If this could be clarified one way or the other on the day it would obviate the need for a further adjournment and inevitable delay. The mother agreed to meet with me and was introduced to me by her lawyer in a small anteroom (that doubled as a cell) which afforded some confidentiality.

Almost from the outset the mother tried to win me over to her position against that of the other professionals. She also took the opportunity to share her views with me concerning my 'paper assessment'. In this she was not being pejorative, or presenting as implacably resistant, but strongly argued her position. She listened carefully to what I had to say and was keen to debate with me the key issues of central importance to the court. Although I engaged in the debate I deflected her attempts to have me take sides; instead I laid out my (therapeutic) position by saying I was interested in knowing more about her family and especially each of the children; how they related to her and each other as well as their individual differences.

I was keen not to become part of the conflict that dominated the relationship between Social Services, the children's guardian and the parents, and had to remind her regularly of this during the session. While she did acknowledge the position I was taking, this process was nevertheless repeated several times throughout this and subsequent sessions. This was a challenge presented by the mother and was the first major therapeutic hurdle to overcome. I was keen to move away from the conflict and engage her in a discussion regarding the family history, especially from the perspective of the children's experience. I wanted to know to what extent she had been able to relate – either at the time or retrospectively – to the children's experience at critical times, especially the domestic violence, their mother's depression and her alcohol misuse, and their enforced separation. I also wanted to consider with her the likely effect that their separation and placement with foster carers had had on each of the children.

The strategy of focusing on the children's experiences and their relational world was valuable in itself but also enabled me to sidestep the conflict with the professionals during this early stage. My approach tended to be curious and caring while attempting to understand the estranged family's relationships from an attachment perspective. Following the difficult first session, in which the mother agreed to continue working with me, the court gave approval for the (therapeutic) assessment to continue.

In the sessions that followed I was struck by how much the mother really enjoyed a debate. She built arguments very effectively and asked searching questions, challenging my views and the views of others. The sessions were conducted in an explorative way with me posing questions often focused on relationships in the family. She engaged well with this approach sometimes choosing the subject matter that was on her mind at that time and/or venting her frustrations in relation to the professionals. We did spend time discussing the ongoing professional conflict, but as the sessions unfolded it was not as dominant a theme, and was often considered alongside my developing understanding of the family's problems, which I had tentatively begun to share with her.

By this stage there was virtually no 'sparring' between us. We had found a way of relating to each other that was to some extent trusting and respectful. We could now discuss even very sensitive family problems. I was aware of a process whereby she had been assessing me as I was assessing her. She was particularly worried about how I might use whatever information she imparted to me in my assessment of her to the court. There was a kind of evolving dual process underway here where I was attempting to build my assessment of the family functioning and the mother's central part in this, while at the same time she was weighing up and testing out to what extent I was competent and trustworthy. This had been a gradual process – though a pivotal time was when I first reported back to the court on the progress I felt we had made up to that time. I had shared everything I intended to put in the report with her beforehand so when she read it with her solicitor there were no unpleasant surprises for her. I wanted her/them to feel part of the assessment process. Following completion of this assessment stage although still pessimistic that the children would be allowed home she could see that I would support such a plan provided progress of the type we had discussed was eventually achieved.

Although still somewhat combative and challenging at times the mother was able (in the sessions with me), by this stage, to critically examine periods and events in the family history in a way she had previously been unable to do. I was (without saying so directly) encouraging and nurturing her ability to be reflective. As the sessions developed the balance gradually shifted from mostly parent–professional conflict and detail in the case history, to the current and future needs of the children. We reviewed each of the children from the perspective of their individual experience and what impact that had on their respective relationships with everyone in the family.

In the course of the discussions with her I was able to share my experience of several similar cases. These were examples where children had been affected by issues such as domestic violence, depression, substance misuse and separation and where they had been later reunited as a family. I shared with her how the parents had eventually been able to acknowledge (on reflection) how absorbed they had been with their own conflict and stress, the intensity of which had temporarily disconnected them from the child's experience, and the potential impact on them. Many parents had also not previously appreciated the extent to which episodes of domestic violence can have a profound effect on children's emotional and psychological well-being. This was something she was largely unaware of. She found this intervention helpful and was by this stage able to explore this kind of very sensitive issue with me and consider to what extent she had been able to relate to the children's experience at these critical times, as well as what difference there might be in the future. We also reviewed what impact the experiences had had on their respective relationships with her. This was a difficult, and at times, painful experience for her, especially as she let down her defences and allowed herself to consider the impact on the emotional and psychological well-being of the children. Out of this discussion she shared with me her fear of losing her attachment with Jane (the youngest child) and that the carer was developing a stronger bond with her the longer they were estranged. She was also able to reflect on a link between this and the negativity she felt for the foster carer.

In the therapeutic relationship I sometimes introduce a psycho-educational element in an attempt to increase parents' knowledge and understanding of something specific (e.g. domestic violence), particularly as it affects children's well-being. Because we are discussing another family, rather than their family, it enables us to step outside the family experience, with all its attendant sensitivity, for a while and generally consider how children might experience a particular context, such as domestic violence, or maternal depression, which was relevant in this case, before later (tentatively) considering the impact these experiences may have had in their family. Using a psycho-educational approach in this way helps to create a general awareness and understanding for the parent of the context itself; it also enables me to assess the parent's capacity to relate to the child-specific experience with each of the children. In this work you have to be respectful of the parent's sensitivity and not to exacerbate unnecessarily feelings of parental guilt and other defensive reactions. This does not mean you avoid sensitive matters, or that overwhelming guilt will not emerge at times; this is almost inevitable. It is more that you set out to strategically manage the situation – acting as emotional scaffolding for them – so that the experience is tolerable and therapeutic.

I find it helpful in these cases to be able to move fluidly between therapy and psycho-educational work according to both the parents' psychological availability and their emotional needs at that time.

By this stage we had reached beyond the mother's hostile defence that had been so dominant earlier. The mother was now engaged and revealing herself to be a very intelligent, thoughtful person with a capacity to be reflective and potentially make changes to her life. She was also able to trust – slowly and gradually – and in doing so she could reflect on past events and experiences without always being angry and defensive. These were qualities that still needed to be nurtured in the context of the therapeutic relationship. She conceded she still used her intelligence to be an 'awkward so and so' with professionals at times.

Undoubtedly this family had gone through a difficult period leading to the removal of the children. We considered how the fact that she did not form a trusting relationship with anyone in Social Services contributed to the enduring nature of the problem. She still considered some professionals were in part to blame and was reluctant to consider her role in the polarised positions that developed.

During the difficult early sessions we had overcome the initial therapeutic obstacles of engagement and building trust. As a result a lot of progress followed. However the relationship between the mother and the social worker (who had removed the children) was still mutually distrustful and conflictual. The court acknowledged the improvement in the case (though the social worker was still resistant) and agreed to a gradual plan of reuniting the family.

The therapeutic assessment had revealed significant attachment problems with each of the children, exacerbated by the prolonged, enforced separation from the parents. Therefore, as part of the process of gradual reunification, we planned to sensitively re-build relationships within the family. This process was undertaken in a graded way over a period of six months. During this time there was a significant improvement in the relationship between the mother and Social Services following a change of social worker. There were still residual problems which surfaced at times, exacerbated by the actions of either side, but these were not insurmountable and resolved without my assistance. As legal proceedings ended and the family were reunited my involvement ceased almost immediately despite the need for further work and consolidation.

Research interview

I met both parents at the family home without the children being present. The reunification had been successful and the family were still together and although two of the oldest children had by now left home and were living independently they were still regularly in contact. The three youngest children were still at home and in school at the time of our meeting. The meeting was very friendly and quite emotional at times and felt a little like a reunion of old friends. Although it was four years since we last met, the issues relevant at the time seemed fresh and alive as we reviewed the experiences. Comparing our respective experiences and perceptions, during that time and since, felt comfortable – almost as if I had remained involved.

It was clear to me the parents' relationship had become stronger since we last met, despite all its problems leading up to and beyond the removal of the children. It seemed that once the tide had turned and there was real belief (or 'hope') on the part of the parents that the children could come home, it galvanised them. They appeared closer and more like a couple than I had seen them in the past. I wondered about a parallel process in which the battle with Social Services to recover the children had enabled them to put on one side their personal/marital conflict. This temporarily subdued rather than resolved problems but the process may have allowed a closer, more conciliatory relationship to develop between them. They agreed the 'fight for the kids' had brought them closer together but they were reluctant to elaborate. At some point in the therapeutic process they had formed an unspoken alliance (for the benefit of the family) that enabled them to have a positive, hopeful focus – whatever their personal historical feelings.

The parents said they realised after a while that I 'had come to help' and not to criticise. I reminded them that the therapy provided a focus on the children – how they had experienced this process and defining their needs, as well as the mother's problems with depression and alcohol. At the core were the parents' significant relationship problems and domestic violence.

I was impressed by their passion for change in the system, especially the way some professionals undertook their work. They talked a great deal about perceived injustices and significant disadvantages for parents to overcome. They reflected a strong sense of powerlessness, anxiety and fear.

The mother said 'I hate the thought of anyone else going through this'.

Both parents felt the experience of losing the children to foster care was profound. Father said – and it was quickly echoed by mother – 'it's the last thing you think of at night and the first thing you think of when you wake up'. Here they were describing feelings of intense anxiety regarding the loss of the children they still re-experience each morning when they awake; slowly as the realisation that the children are home is confirmed in their conscious mind, and the family are together, the anxiety slowly dissipates. Alongside the anxiety is the feeling of residual anger toward some professionals who the parents identified as very unhelpful.

They felt they needed help earlier in the process. 'You are aware of a mental battle'.

When the father in particular said this, I was able to say that I wasn't sure if he resented my involvement during the early stages. We were able to discuss this freely and for the first time he said that he felt the individual sessions I had with his wife were helpful. They felt that my role in mediating with the professional system was significant and achieved some progress at a critical time, giving them 'some hope'.

The father said: 'you believed us and believed in us'.

There were lots of comments from them reflecting the conflict with professionals. While they conceded they were architects of their own misfortune to some extent they also referred to their perception of professional incompetence and misconduct. This did not simply represent externalised negativity on their part, as the original social worker in the case had been dismissed. Like many families in these circumstances they referred to feeling 'powerless' as if their word was easily dismissed while the professionals tended to be accepted. They clearly felt as intensely now about the perceived injustice as they did then.

'They can be two-faced – you can't beat them'. 'What they say is law'. 'Some social workers are better than others'.

The parents complained of what they described as 'selected reporting'. In this they felt that what they said and how they said it, in formal and informal meetings with professionals, was turned against them and sometimes misrepresented.

The mother said: 'I don't trust anyone anymore'. This was said with some passion but is strictly speaking not accurate, because they had trusted some people in the professional system. I pointed out they had trusted me and their lawyers and slowly and gradually other professionals. They agreed that the statement was not completely accurate, but I felt the saying of it had enabled them to vent intense, historical feelings of anger, which although not disabling them now, were still not completely resolved.

Their most positive comments were saved for their legal representatives. 'We had good lawyers'. They were 'sensitive as well as good'.

They were highly critical of the social worker, the children's guardian and the psychologist who had assessed them during the legal proceedings. They now felt vindicated because they had proved they could be successfully reunited as a family.

Reflecting on my involvement the mother said:

'With you I could say something – you didn't tell me what to do'. 'We talked about everything'. She indicated that I valued her opinion and that she felt with others she was 'always fighting to be heard'.

I was able to remind her of how difficult our early relationship had been with her trying to pull me into the conflict. She agreed but grew to like the way we discussed rather than battled with issues. Father, who had some idea of how his wife was battling with the professionals at that time said:

'They should have brought you in earlier'. 'We needed to sit and reflect and do things differently' with Social Services. 'Only you told us what was in the report'; with other professionals 'we did not know what they would write. We complained about the children's guardian and the psychologist but it made no difference'.

Mother felt the professionals were dictating to them what should happen as well as what to do, which she resented. 'Whatever we did was wrong – they (SSD) wanted us to separate'. This gave me an opportunity to comment on how well they seemed together, appearing much more resilient and cohesive as a couple now than when I was originally involved. It seemed the advice from Social Services to separate had paradoxically made them more determined to remain together.

They described feeling shamed and disrespected by the process – as if they were criminals – especially in formal meetings and at court.

With so many professionals to see and seemingly endless assessments they described 'going through the motions' each time and 'losing hope'. They said the process was confusing and they 'did not understand the different roles of professionals'. Father who had a particularly difficult relationship with the children's guardian said 'I think the children's guardian has too much power'. The father went on to say he had a fantasy of bi-passing the professionals and:

'Talking with the Judge – just the two of us' – in an attempt to magic some solution between them and prevent numerous adjournments and appearances in court where he said 'I felt humiliated'.

They stated how the children were harmed by the separation from each other as well as the parents. 'They came back changed and not for the better'. There were 'lots of temper tantrums' and 'in care they were given lots of material benefits that we could not provide'. On their return the parents described how the older children:

'Used being in foster care against us to get their own way'. 'It's been hard work'.

The parents felt the numerous meetings with Social Services did not help and often made matters worse. The children often attended their reviews and then later would run off from their placements 'and they (Social Services) would blame us'.

Responding to the question 'do you think you have changed?' was difficult for them. It was clear to me they had changed in their attitude to professionals and their own relationship appeared far closer than at the outset. They also referred to being wary, even suspicious of professionals early on until they felt they could trust them – though never completely. They found it difficult to elaborate on their self-understanding when discussing it together. It seemed to me to reflect that a certain amount of defensiveness still remained for them – perhaps subconsciously fearing closer examination of some of the history may threaten their new-found relationship. I was naturally respectful of this and careful not to pursue this as a therapy session. When I contacted the current social worker prior to the research interview he confirmed significant changes in the parents' attitude and was generally positive about them. He interestingly had engaged with the mother's need to debate matters sometimes at length and felt it enhanced their relationship.

My role ceased at the point of rehabilitation where the family were mostly left to their own devices. They were successfully reunited to the extent that the children did not return to care. They remained a family with problems and would have benefitted from ongoing help, especially in repairing the damage caused by the enforced separation. Problems of the same magnitude that led to the children's removal however did not reoccur. The parents' relationship appeared to have strengthened during the second half of my involvement (without any direct couple work) in the case and then consolidated over time. I wondered if the developing therapeutic relationship between the mother and myself, and in particular the reflective space away from the professional conflict, had indirectly positively affected their personal relationship.

The parents in this case demonstrated that while they could be very challenging for professionals and often uncooperative, they could cope as a family if a suitable context was created allowing them to engage with appropriate help and support. This is far from easy and I am not underestimating the challenge for professionals, especially undertaking statutory responsibilities in these cases.

Seeing the parents again I was careful not to expose therapeutic issues and then leave them vulnerable without ongoing support. It had been gratifying to know they had remained a family and the interview felt like a mutually beneficial experience.

CASE 2 – The Bevan Family

Case background and professional concerns

Craig was the youngest of three children in this family and had been diagnosed with ADHD by the local CAMHS and prescribed medication. His mother had mild learning difficulties and a history of being sexually abused by her older brother when she was a child. Both parents had a history of substance and alcohol misuse for many years pre-dating the arrival of their family. Following a very violent dispute between the parents and a neighbour that escalated to involve the children in the encounter, the family were made homeless for a short time. At this point the two older children were cared for by relatives, but because of Craig's problems he was placed in foster care at that time, ostensibly until the parents were re-housed. The middle child was returned to the family when they were re-housed in another area while the oldest child remained with the grandmother, having settled well there.

Craig's behaviour in foster care deteriorated following the separation from his family leading to a series of foster placement (four) breakdowns in a

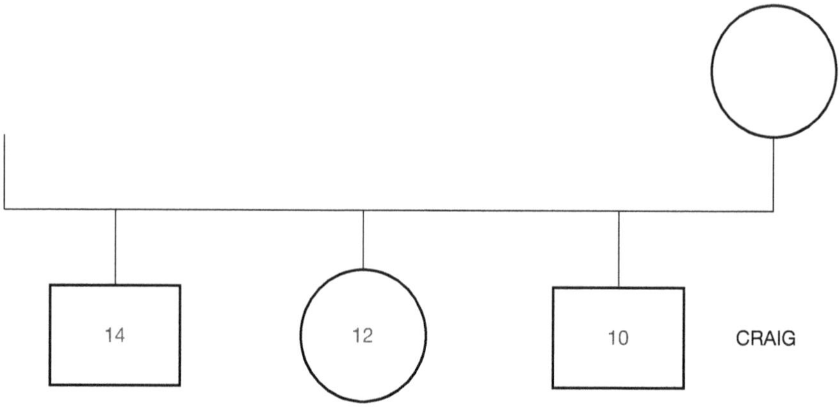

Figure 4.2 Case 2 – The Bevan Family

relatively short space of time. Although in his fifth placement and experiencing a period of stable care his parents were by now considered not able enough to provide him with good enough care should he be returned to them. This change of perception of the parents' capacity to cope with him was due in large part to the series of placement breakdowns that had taken place. By this stage Craig was perceived to be a very disturbed boy with complex needs that his parents would be unable to meet. This perception of the parents' ability to cope was challenged by the parents who felt Craig's considerable problems had been compounded by his separation from them and a traumatic succession of placement breakdowns. During the Social Services assessment they discovered mother had learning difficulties as well as some mental health problems with anxiety and periodic depression. Their view was that the parents, especially the mother, were unable to cope with Craig's complex and demanding behaviours and his developmental needs. The family acknowledged Craig had complex needs and they needed help in coping with him, but beyond that disputed much of the detail of the Social Services assessment. The parents and the Social Services were unable to resolve their different perceptions of the problems and became locked in seemingly intractable disagreement. The lack of any meaningful dialogue between the social worker and the parents resulted in an impasse and inevitable legal proceedings.

Summary of sessions

From the outset, I found the parents relatively easy to engage including discussing the sensitive issues that were central in this case. They were both keen to have Craig back in the family as soon as possible and felt they could manage him – though they were also keen to improve their ability to parent him and receive whatever help they could. They felt guilty he was still in foster care while his siblings were home. They acknowledged he had significant problems but felt strongly that a series of placement breakdowns and the enforced separation from his family had compounded the difficulties and damaged relationships between them. The mother also openly acknowledged to me she had not been a competent or confident parent and had become over-dependent on her husband to care for the children. She lacked confidence generally and was periodically depressed and felt guilty that the father had to take much more of the parental responsibility than would otherwise be necessary.

She had been employed from time to time and contributed to the family income but recognised she had to some extent tended to avoid a fuller parental role and had become more and more dependent on her husband to do that for both of them.

It emerged in the early work that both parents, mother in particular, were keen to have parenting skills training that was not (as provided by Social Services) group orientated but tailored more to their specific difficulties. They appeared to understand that this kind of intervention involved a lot of work on their part to acquire the necessary competence as well scrutiny of their efforts to confirm the success or otherwise of the intervention. Although the mother had mild or borderline learning difficulties her history of depression and childhood sexual abuse had greater significance as this had affected her emotional availability to Craig at times. From the history it appeared she had probably not 'bonded' effectively with him compared to the older children and he was insecurely attached to her. This aspect seemed to have fundamentally influenced their relationship and formed the basis of much of the therapeutic work with the family. Mother's history of depression and abuse has also influenced the development of their respective parental roles – with father being authoritative and therefore central, and mother having little authority, as peripheral.

With the parents we developed a common understanding of the core problems and then co-constructed a plan intending to address the various areas of concern identified by them and Social Services. We agreed there were specific parenting issues intrinsic to caring for a child with Craig's difficulties that would be central to the plan. Also, we agreed to review their parental roles as well as re-build the relationship with Craig that had been damaged by the enforced separation. Alongside this, the mother wanted help from a female therapist to address the issues arising from the sexual abuse she experienced as a child. From this point I worked closely with a female associate who focused on this work as well as assisting with the parenting skills training.

The parents engaged well with the parenting programme we devised and were more able to work collaboratively by the end, acknowledging father's greater competence, but with the mother much more involved than previously. The mother was supported in becoming more centrally involved in parenting as well as gradually re-building her relationship with Craig. However, this proved to be challenging as Craig had considerable resentment toward his parents blaming them for his enforced separation from the family. Whereas his parents blamed

Social Services for the separation, Craig openly blamed his parents. Even when this aspect improved Craig was often ambivalent toward his parents. This tended to undermine the mother's self-confidence in particular and hinder progress. Although progress was made in these areas very gradually and eventually reached 'good enough' in parenting terms, there were setbacks from time to time and it remained very much a 'work in progress' for them.

We worked steadily with them on the parenting programme as well as providing therapy for the mother for six months before gradually reuniting them over a period of a further three months. They were a family with significant problems and needed ongoing support from Social Services and other agencies following our involvement in order to remain 'good enough' parents. The reunification was successful but Craig's deeply felt resentment at the enforced separation from his family remained an issue as did his fear of being taken back into care. This had the effect of undermining mother's self-confidence and authority with Craig.

In this case the therapeutic work moved fluidly between providing parenting skills and dealing with individual therapeutic issues related to the mother's past as they arose. Although initially reticent the mother was gradually able to confront many of the therapeutic issues from her past and ultimately benefit from doing so. These changes in the mother were brought about in the context of a trusting (therapeutic) relationship. In attachment terms, the therapeutic relationship acted as a temporary 'secure base' for her and provided a holding and supportive function for her as she negotiated a difficult period of transition in her life. When our involvement ended I was concerned she remained vulnerable without ongoing support and therapy especially as Craig's problems would be long term.

The research interview

When I contacted the parents to enlist their cooperation for the research interview I was heartened to learn that the rehabilitation plan had worked. It was three years since my involvement and the oldest boy was now in the army and the daughter was living close by in her own accommodation. Craig had remained in their care despite significant problems at times. The parents were pleased to report a better relationship with the current social worker who had been very supportive of them. This was significant because there had been considerable conflict with the previous social worker leading up to Craig's return to the family.

Both parents still felt the enforced separation from Craig and subsequent placement breakdowns were key events in their case and had made matters worse. They felt very stressed at the time and although Craig had remained with his parents they had often struggled to cope. On reflection they felt Craig's return to their care had been more difficult than they expected after such a long period of separation.

Craig was much more insecure and at times resentful toward them making it more difficult to manage him than before he was taken into foster care. Following Craig's return home he felt for a long time he would be returned to care despite reassurances from his parents and professionals to the contrary.

He was ambivalent at times; happy he was home but resenting the time he had been away.

Both parents benefitted from a change of social worker. The mother said: 'It's taken a long time – but I trust Malcolm' (current social worker). The previous social worker 'told him (referring to the children's father) to leave me – they saw me as the problem'.

Both parents really resented the way the Social Services had encouraged them to separate; the Social Services view was that the father could provide a better home for the children without the mother. Both parents acknowledged some responsibility for events leading up to Craig's placement with foster carers, as well as remaining in care when the other children had already returned home. They felt guilty about this, as well as being unable to cope at that time. Overall they felt the intervention of Social Services had contributed to making matters worse for them as a family. The legal proceedings had been a very stressful experience for them and they still felt anxious, angry and resentful whenever they reflected on that time.

In response to the question about whether they have 'changed' the mother reflected on the disclosure and subsequent therapy in relation to her experience of sexual abuse. The mother was very positive about the therapy she received; she had learned to be more positive about herself and importantly had learned to 'trust' in the course of the therapy. Learning to trust was a positive theme for both of them. The father felt they had changed as a family after receiving help from us; this following a very difficult period when they appeared to be fragmenting.

They indicated the (therapeutic) involvement with them offered 'hope' for them at a critical time as well as an opportunity to build some trust.

From the outset they acknowledged they had problems as a family especially in managing Craig's ADHD. They were not alone in this as four of his foster placements had broken down demonstrating the challenging nature of his behaviour. They had asked Social Services for help but their perception is they did not receive anything meaningful. The mother was also critical of the adult mental health service; reflecting on that time she said: 'I wanted to talk, not take tablets'.

The mother felt she was being 'judged' by childcare and adult mental health professionals and seen as the source of the 'problem'. She described feeling angry because of this and how it undermined her confidence and self-esteem.

They did not feel they were listened to by professionals. They felt coerced into attending a group-based parenting class, prior to my involvement. They found it quite helpful in a general way though it did not address the specific parenting problems of caring for Craig. Craig's difficulties were now more complex and were as much about attachment issues and residual resentment as they were about his behaviour and ADHD.

We discussed reaching the impasse that led to legal proceedings. The Social Services' view acknowledged Craig had significant problems, confirmed by four foster placement breakdowns, but saw the problem as parental (particularly maternal) incompetence; they considered this view was supported by the lack of perceived progress following the parenting classes. The classes did provide some limited benefit though the parents felt they did not address the fundamental issues for the mother – which were therapeutic as well as parenting skills.

She said: 'I needed someone to talk to' (about issues of abuse and her lack of self-esteem). 'When you ask for help they don't give it to you'. Father said 'we needed someone to work with us together', as well as the mother's individual problems. 'You could see Craig had special problems', 'we felt you understood'. 'You should have been brought in earlier'.

The mother said: 'I have been abused – they made me feel I was to blame'. 'They were punishing me for being (mentally) ill and depressed'. She had mild learning difficulties and struggled to express her feelings coherently at times. As she became more and more frustrated she could get angry and was perceived by some professionals as being threatening and aggressive. The mother had found the whole experience extremely stressful and she consequently struggled to make relationships with professionals.

She said that while she experienced me as understanding she could (understandably) not talk to me about the abuse. She spoke of the benefit she received from the involvement with a female therapist. I reminded them that we had worked out the therapeutic plan together. They confirmed by that collaborating with them in this way we had made the therapy relevant for them.

It was also evident that adopting a flexible, therapeutic approach that allowed us to move fluidly between providing individual therapy for the mother and specific parenting skills training, was also very helpful.

The parents were willing to participate in the research interview as they did not want other parents to go through a similar experience. They referred to having tried to help other parents in their community when they were in similar circumstances but without success; they said very profoundly: 'It is hard to pass on your experience (losing your child to foster care) to others'; implying that some parents have to unfortunately experience this for themselves before appreciating the reality of the consequences for their family.

CASE 3 – The Morris Family

Case background and professional concerns

The Morris family has four children aged two, four, eight and ten who were removed from their parents' care following serious episodes of domestic

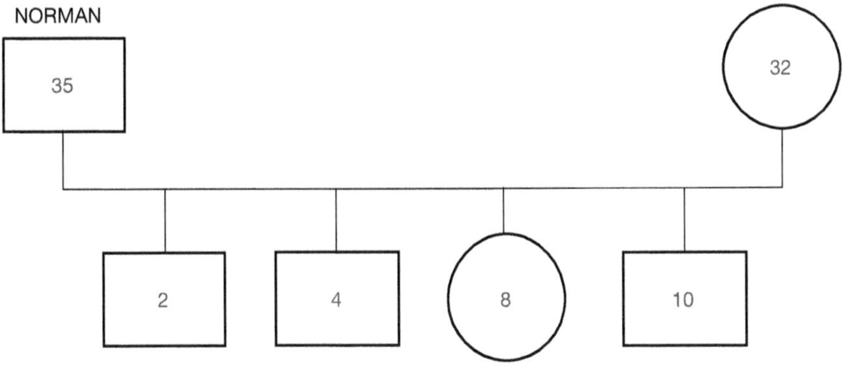

Figure 4.3 Case 3 – The Morris Family

violence, concerns over the father's misuse of drugs and alcohol, the mother's inability to protect the children, and the parents' minimisation of professionals' concerns and non-cooperation with Social Services. The children were initially placed together with a maternal aunt who subsequently abused them before being placed (oldest and youngest together; two middle children together) with foster carers. The parents had separated for a while after being advised to do so by Social Services but then reunited. After a very low point when the father had lived rough on the streets he claimed to have had an 'epiphany' experience in which he acknowledged his culpability and responsibility for events leading up to the removal of the children. He consequently became drug free and reunited with the mother. Despite Social Services advice to remain separated they became committed to fighting to have the children returned to their joint care.

Summary of sessions

By the time of my involvement there was some support among the other Experts for returning the children to the parents' care but there were concerns about the stability of the parents' relationship in the longer term and their ability to maintain any improvement. Since being separated from the children and following a very difficult period apart, the parents' relationship had appeared to stabilise. My role was to try and engage the parents, the father in particular, in therapeutic work and support them toward being reunited with the children if that were possible. If the children could be returned to the parents' care, the process was expected to present the family with serious challenges even though they had demonstrated commitment and made some progress.

I knew that relationships between the children and their parents had suffered during the enforced separation; firstly as a result of the abuse suffered while in the care of their aunt; secondly because family life had been unstable as a result of domestic violence and substance misuse prior to being placed with their aunt. The two oldest children were ambivalent and at times resentful toward the parents, blaming them for the separation, which had been traumatic. During the assessment phase I had agreed with the parents that we would focus on the quality of relationships within the family especially given the background of substance misuse and domestic violence that pre-dated the separation. As the work unfolded it became clear that the two oldest children's relationship with the parents, father in particular, had been seriously damaged during the period of the separation. The relationship between the parents and the children needed to be gradually re-built while addressing the secondary attachment issues that had arisen following the traumatic separation.

The mother was very friendly and easily engaged. The father was very direct, challenging and at times combative in his approach. He was easily emotionally aroused and frequently used expletives though not directly at me. He was aware others described him as threatening and aggressive at times but he insisted he did not mean what he said to be taken personally. However, I could see how some professionals would feel very uncomfortable with him when he was aroused.

Most of the work I did with the family was with the father. Despite his belligerence at times he became engaged with me and very interested in what I had to contribute. He thoroughly enjoyed discussions and loved an argument. He is an extremely intelligent man assessed as having an I.Q. of 140 by the clinical psychologist who had seen him for a psychological assessment. He was very quick thinking, logical and often rigorous in his approach to discussing problems. He had diligently read and understood the paperwork relating to the case as well as relevant literature, including sometimes the most recent research. He would take account of what others said in any argument though sometimes it felt like being cross-examined. Many professionals are not used to parents challenging and debating with them in this way and may feel very uncomfortable and intimidated by his quick thinking. Indeed I found I had to be prepared to engage in a rigorous, intense debate with him at times – acknowledging and respecting his argument and at the same time avoid becoming defensive.

Although the parents' relationship with the social worker had been troubled they had a good relationship with an experienced support worker who supported the mother (following the domestic violence) in particular and helped them improve aspects of their parenting. She was very clear and direct in her approach and both parents held her in some regard. The support worker and I were able to work together on this case so that our respective interventions were complementary. The parents needed help with understanding the nature of the relationship problems within the family; this included their relationship as well as the relationship they had with each of the children. It was acknowledged by this stage that the relationships between the parents and the children had been affected by many factors including: the parents' past behaviour; the abuse the children suffered while cared for by an aunt; and the enforced separation.

The relationship problems between the children and the parents differed across the age groups. The two youngest children did not understand at a cognitive level much of what had happened but had been very distressed by the abuse, disruption and separation from each other as well as their parents. During contact sessions and the process of reunification the children tended to act out the consequences of these experiences with very demanding, distressing behaviours. The oldest two children, who understood far more of what had happened, were more challenging and frequently reminded the parents directly as well as indirectly of their anger and resentment concerning the abuse and enforced separation; often saying directly that it was all due to the parents and their behaviour. The two oldest children were very intelligent and understood to some extent the reasons for being in care and were able to say directly to their father: 'If you weren't such a junkie' or 'because you and mam used to fight' we were in care.

On hearing remarks such as these the father felt overwhelmed with guilt that effectively undermined his attempts to regain parental authority with them. Dealing with the parents' feelings of guilt and attempting to re-establish (and enhance) their relationships with the children became a central focus of the therapeutic work. The parents' relationship itself had stabilised by this time making it easier to create a secure, predictable, emotional experience for the children and improving each of their attachments. All four children had regressed to some extent and were more challenging and demanding than prior to their removal from the family home.

Father was quickly able to understand the attachment issues from an intellectual position. It took somewhat longer to translate the understanding into a way of behaving and relating with the children that generated the secure attachment experience for them. We had targeted achieving a 'secure attachment' with each of the children as the ultimate goal in our work together. The father, more than the mother, was periodically visited by intense, almost overwhelming feelings of guilt – occasionally leading to incapacity and brief bouts of depression. At other times he would externalise his negative feelings, often aiming them in the convenient direction of Social Services.

As we neared the end of the reunification process the father was involved in a violent incident with a neighbour who (while heavily intoxicated) had accidentally, but quite seriously hurt one of the younger children. The father became very angry when he found out and assaulted the neighbour. The Police were involved and informed Social Services. The father, while very much regretting his behaviour became concerned the reunification process would be affected. As a result of this and with the agreement of the professionals involved we agreed to do some 'anger management' work. He was highly motivated at this stage and grasped the concept of anger management very quickly and worked hard to achieve ways of being able to regulate his intense emotional arousal (often triggered by shame) at critical times. As a result of this improvement he also began to manage his relationship with Social Services more effectively which was a bi-product of the anger management intervention.

The parents at this stage were aware that they needed to be significantly better than just 'good enough' parents because of the complex, individual and collective needs of the children. The father's resentment would surface at times as he oscillated between blaming the aunt, Social Services and then himself for the children's 'dreadful ordeal'. The mother had dealt better with the historical issues and by now mostly engaged well with the professionals, benefitting from the help and support she received. Untangling the complex history and the part played by everyone in this family's breakup, and the intense feelings it generated, was an important focus of the therapy – much more so with the father than the mother.

The father was very strong on concepts and as long as he engaged in conversation it was possible to help him understand issues. He also became more reflective having experienced the benefit during the months of therapy. The professionals and the court were pleased he had clearly accepted responsibility for the critical events in the past and maintained his commitment to a new lifestyle following his epiphany.

The therapeutic work and reunification process took about six months following which my involvement with the family ceased. I was aware there were still significant problems in the family that would leave them vulnerable and their future stability uncertain.

The research interview

The father (referred to here as Norman), agreed to participate in the research interview and we met at the family home. The family were still together and had survived despite problems – though not of the magnitude that led to their removal. On reflection, Norman still felt he was the main cause of the children's removal from the family home. He viewed his substance misuse and the episodic domestic violence to be largely his responsibility. He was nevertheless angry with the social workers for the way they undertook their role and how they treated him and his family prior to and post removal of the children. He quoted several examples whereby he felt: 'They moved the goal posts' or were 'disingenuous' with him.

He remained very angry at the way Social Services placed the children with their aunt, despite the parents' protest, and where they were subsequently abused by her. He warned them in advance of the dangers of the placement and what she was like – but they did not believe him. He now feels the children were more damaged by the placement with their aunt than they were at home with them with all their problems.

It was only after the children were removed did he begin to come to terms with the realities: 'You cannot fight the system but have to make it work for you'.

When I asked him about whether he had changed and how? He talked about being able to deal with professionals: 'You gave me more tools which helped'. 'I had to learn – never mind the psychosis in my head . . . I had to assess each question from the professionals and ask myself – what have I got to do? . . . I just wanted my children back'.

He recalled some aspects of therapy that he found useful: 'You helped me relate to professionals as a means to an end rather than treating each interaction as a personal affront'.

He recalled the advice on managing young children's insecure attachment behaviour and repeated to me the core content of the 'anger management' work we had undertaken together: 'You did not patronise me. . . Treated me like an intelligent human being. . .You were conversational, you debated with me.'

Norman acknowledged he is inclined toward being anti-authority in attitude and disliked professionals being critical and directive of him; he has an awareness of this now as an unresolved legacy from his own childhood. Something that is a work in progress for him. What made the difference or was a turning point? 'When I realised we are good parents if I stop behaving like a teenager' (referring to his drug and alcohol use). He was still angry that the social worker had advised the children's mother to leave him so she could have the children back.

The turning point for them was when they separated for a while and the father lived rough on the streets. Norman had his 'epiphany' experience before getting back together to fight to have all the children returned so they could be a family again. The 'epiphany' experience also led to him giving up drugs and restricting alcohol. He slowly and gradually learnt to engage better – firstly with non-statutory professionals – and attended various courses on domestic violence and substance misuse. The course on 'minimising' and domestic violence had a major influence on him and was one of several turning points.

He felt the statutory professionals were generally disrespectful to him even when it was established he was very intelligent with a superior IQ (140). 'Once the social worker was clear with me that my drug-taking is a threat to the children – I gave it up there and then, whatever my beliefs.'

We reflected on the time when he began accepting the responsibility for his actions including culpability for what had happened to the children even though there were other significant factors. He said 'we were treated harshly (by SSD) but it was not a good environment for children' . . . I realised I had been minimising' – a direct quote from the domestic violence course he attended. 'It gave me another perspective.'

'I was antagonistic . . . It got better once I stopped taking it personally' (with professionals). 'I started dealing with it better – I went to County Hall for a meeting and conducted myself properly . . . They were all shocked'.

'I feel so guilty . . . I was left with nothing . . . I was treated like an abuser, an idiot – but I've got to take responsibility for this . . . I had a mantra – cast these devils aside.'

'I trusted and believed you – I can remember what you said to me about anger management – you said "zero tolerance for violence".'

'I think the (professional) system should weigh things up better – it's too easy just to take them (the children) than to work it out. They want you to admit they were right.'

Responding to the question of whether he had changed and how, he said:

'You've got to listen – in the end we needed to change and we did.'

'I know I've changed . . . I've tried to help other parents in the same situation. I say you've got to listen and take what they say seriously – they have power.'

'It is hard to get them to benefit from your experience . . . I learned the hard way.'

Although referring mostly to behavioural and lifestyle issues Norman was able to reflect on 'change' at different levels: as an individual, as a parent, and as a couple. He referred to the influence of my work and that of the domestic violence course he attended. Being treated with dignity was important to him as was respecting his undoubted intellectual ability, which once positively engaged became a positive factor.

CASE 4 – The Knight Family

Case background and professional concerns

This case involved very young parents who had three children before they were 20 years of age. They were struggling to cope from the outset and without

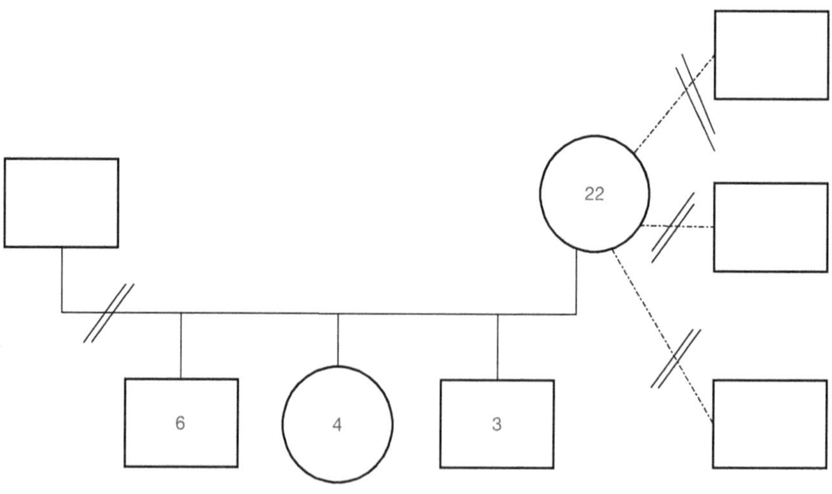

Figure 4.4 Case 4 – The Knight Family

any support from either of their families soon had relationship problems themselves, leading to their separation. Following the breakup of the parents' relationship the mother embarked on a series of relationships with other much older men who she allowed to move into the family home after only knowing them a short time. The mother was dominated and frequently abused by these men, placing the children's safety and well-being at risk in the process. These relationships broke down very quickly sometimes in a matter of weeks with only a short gap before she had another man move into the family home.

Sheila, the mother, feared being alone and was desperate to recruit a replacement partner each time a relationship broke down. This was a very unstable period for the family when domestic violence and neglect had prevailed with the children experiencing 'significant harm'. The pattern of abusive partners moving in and then out to be replaced by another had reached a point where it was seemingly beyond Sheila's control.

The children were removed following a period of intense professional concern and placed (two youngest together, the oldest child alone) with foster carers. The first placement for the oldest child broke down following allegations of abuse against the carers and eventually all three were placed together in a very stable placement in which they all thrived.

Summary of sessions

When I first met the mother she was quite shy, reticent and unassertive. This changed as she gradually began to understand my role and relate to me and gain in confidence. She slowly engaged and as she did so she conveyed a sense of her commitment to the (therapeutic) process and wanting to meet whatever demands were required of her for the children's return to her care. During the various assessments that took place, including my own, she accepted responsibility for what had happened and did not attach any blame to anyone else. At times she looked almost overwhelmed with the seriousness of the situation and the extent of professional involvement in her life. She struggled to deal with all of this and looked anxiously to professionals for support and direction.

As the sessions with me unfolded and the mother gained in confidence it became clear she was an intelligent young woman who was still anxious, immature and very vulnerable. Sheila had been overwhelmed by the whole experience; firstly being left on her own with three children after their father left home; then later with a succession of partners and intense professional concern. The overwhelming nature of this experience had caused her to retreat within herself, looking to others to take charge on her behalf. She feared being alone and for a time found herself depending on a series of temporary, unsuitable partners she had acquired almost in desperation.

As a result of the protracted legal proceedings and intense professional involvement in her life Sheila had learned a great deal about what others expected of her. As she began to feel supported she gradually changed her attitude and approach to the role of parenting. She became highly motivated to have the children back despite the considerable obstacles. She was aware she needed to develop more effective parenting skills as well as refraining from engaging in short-term relationships that were potentially harmful to the children as well as herself. Following a period of assessment we agreed to focus on the following areas:

- Her perception of personal relationships and stages of closeness leading to intimacy and/or commitment.
- Her perception of parent–child relationships and in particular her children's need for a secure attachment experience.
- Enhancing mother's 'sense of self' in relation to the above, especially her confidence and self-identity as a mother.

The initial work of engaging Sheila had gone very well. She demonstrated an interest and commitment to understanding her past difficulties and to being more protective of the children and meeting their needs in the future. As she gained self-confidence her real personality and intelligence emerged; she gradually became more able to consider ideas, reflect on experiences, and consider new possibilities for herself. She demonstrated a capacity for insight and self-understanding I would not have anticipated at the outset. In this supportive therapeutic context she began to blossom as an individual; her new-found self-esteem and confidence was increasingly apparent to other professionals who were involved in the case.

She was able to bring this same attitude and new self-confidence into the parenting programme that had been specifically developed for her. She struggled to cope with the demands of the children early in the programme but persevered. With a lot of support and practice her parenting skills gradually improved; she developed confidence and authority with the children as they responded positively to her parenting. As a result of this, she was able to re-build her relationship with each of the children. We used the contact sessions with the children to practice her new skills and meet her developing needs as a parent; gradually in this way she was able to build and upgrade her skills. Over a period of six months there was considerable improvement in her parental competences, stamina to cope as a single parent, and general management of three young children.

As Sheila progressed the contact sessions with the children were extended and adapted so that they increasingly represented the demands of every day family life. The children's foster carer was very helpful and invited her into her home to observe life in the foster home. Experiencing their mother and foster carer getting on well was extremely valuable to the children who then did not have a sense of divided loyalty as they coped with the transition period before returning to their mother's care.

Sheila had benefitted greatly from the influence of the foster carer. This experience demonstrated the value of a mentor or role model for Sheila so she could build on the progress she had made once they were together as a family again. Unfortunately the foster carer lived a long way from the family home although was able to offer some support to Sheila by phone. When Sheila was re-housed she discovered she was close to an aunt who was interested in supporting them. As progress was made toward the final stages of reunification the mother became more assertive, confidently expressing her views with professionals. She did not now look overwhelmed and dependent and had a much clearer sense of her own identity and purpose.

Sheila had decided that she could not have a partner herself while fighting to have the children returned to her care. We had considered the nature of her previous relationships, which she now understood in relation to her low self-esteem and anxiety at that time. She saw the relationships as harmful for her as well as the children and as representing a short-term solution to her (at that time) overwhelming fear of being alone. We discussed the part played by 'trust' in the stages of a relationship. We referred to 'picking a good one' – meaning someone, not anyone who was respectful and committed to her and the children for the right reasons. She, and the children had needs to be considered in this process of gradually becoming familiar with each other. Of paramount consideration was the protection of the children, which she now clearly understood. Sheila's self-understanding and capacity to be appropriately relational in her life was a central focus of the therapeutic work.

Once the family were reunited my involvement ceased almost immediately. While I was very pleased with Sheila's progress I was concerned she was very young and vulnerable. Although the full-time demands of childcare would be a challenge for her the next real test would be how she responded when confronted with a potentially exploitative relationship.

The research interview

When we met at Sheila's home for the interview it had been more than three years since the last session. Sheila had a new partner and another child in that time. Both the partner and the new child were present for the session and they seemed like a settled family. Sheila wanted to show off not only how she had established stability for her family but that she had been able to 'pick a good one' and avoid exploitative partners. They had been together for two and a half years and looked very happy. Sheila appeared so much more mature, confident and content within herself in marked contrast to when we first met. She comfortably recalled the history of the case with me and shared her recollections in front of her partner who she said 'knows it all'.

'In the beginning everything and everyone seemed against me . . . Martin (new social worker) was a breath of fresh air – he worked for us to be back together.' The previous social worker had been taken off the case after being criticised by the Judge.

This was one of several turning points identified by Sheila. Others were when the Judge seemed to be supportive of her in court and she felt she was being heard, as well as when (on my recommendation), she had extended contact with her children in the community with 'no supervision'. She said: 'It was unreal to begin with but it felt more like being a family . . . I felt I was being trusted.'

The foster carers who had the children prior to their return home were 'excellent' according to Sheila. She said 'they looked after the children – they did so much . . . They were helped there rather than damaged . . . The previous carer (for the oldest child) lied and the children were harmed . . . Once I knew they were settled (in placement) I could concentrate on the court case . . . You improved contact allowing me to do more with the children.'

On reflection this was a challenge she felt she rose to very well and this enabled her to develop confidence and self-belief. She learned a great deal from the foster carers who were very fond of her and allowed her to visit the children in their home. This new supportive (therapeutic) context involving the foster carers enabled Sheila to grow and become increasingly self-confident. When I asked her if she had changed she said very profoundly – 'yes, you can see it in my kids'. By this she meant the children looked so much more content and settled.

'I got to know myself . . . I kept reminding myself why I was doing this . . . Believing in myself – saying I can do it . . . I kept repeating this to myself.'

'What is your priority – don't get too negative' (with professionals).

'The hardest thing was for me not to get into battles – so much to disagree with in court. Not to get too down.'

Sheila was giving herself inspiring and supportive messages so that she did not give in and become completely overwhelmed. Court was very difficult for her especially in the earlier stages.

'The way I got through it was saying (after a lot of personal criticism in court): OK this was not so good, but . . . then find something positive in the experience'. This was easier once she felt supported by professionals who had been previously critical or ambivalent toward her.

'A lot of good has come out of this – I am closer to my (birth) family now.' She had reached an understanding with them after experiencing conflict and disappointment with them for several years.

'I am pleased I got on well with all of you by the end.' Sheila felt professionals had a regard for her and the progress she had made by the end of the case.

'In the beginning I believed nobody wanted to help me . . . Relationship-wise I was going from loser to loser . . . I always thought I needed someone and couldn't bear to be without a partner.'

'I had to use what I learned . . . Not to go from zero to 10 [a relationship score measuring closeness and trust] overnight and putting my kids at risk . . . I kept saying to myself I put it wrong, now I'm going to put it right . . . You must never give up on yourself if you know you can do something.'

'The children were my motivation and the court case helped.' Sheila acknowledged her own culpability and responsibility.

'I thought the Judge was tough but fair . . . Going into the courtroom was the hardest part of everything . . . Listening to professionals' views of me and my care of the children as if I wasn't there – I wanted to scream out – I'm here you know . . . I felt like a criminal.'

'My barrister was a big influence . . . He was realistic but encouraging . . . It was 85% positive by the end.'

Responding to: what advice would you give to other parents in similar circumstances? 'Listen to advice – get to know yourself – follow your heart (she looked toward the children), and find out what's your priority.'

I was struck by how much self-development had taken place for Sheila, inspired a great deal by the quality of her own internal dialogue which had developed as the work unfolded. She had got to 'know herself' and was now able to be insightful and reflective. Moreover she now understands her own as well as the relationship needs of the children.

CASE 5 – The Wilson Family

Case background and professional concerns

Jean, the mother in this case was very young (19 years) and vulnerable when she gave birth to her son. Her birth family history was characterised by disruption, conflict, and rejection – especially from her mother who she had seen little of since she was ten years old. Her teenage years were mostly spent in residential care as well as a lengthy period in an in-patient psychiatric unit. She had spent periods 'on the run' while still in care and then later having left care she was homeless at various times. She had been raped by a stranger when she was 13 years old having absconded from her children's home at that time.

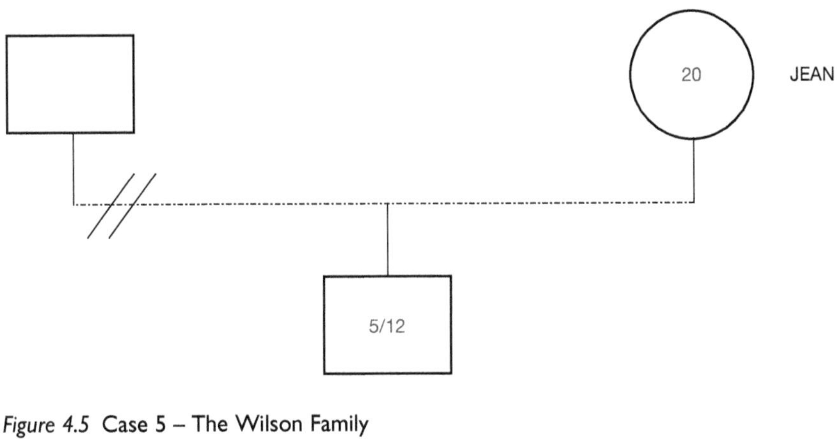

Figure 4.5 Case 5 – The Wilson Family

Jean was a regular drug user and frequently in trouble with the police because of violent behaviour.

When she realised she was pregnant at 19 years of age it was unplanned and came as a great shock to her. Shortly after that she became drug free and made significant changes to her lifestyle. As she had virtually no support system at that time she was placed in a mother and baby unit following the birth of her son. Unfortunately in the midst of the legal proceedings, which were under way by that stage she walked out of the placement after a dispute with the staff, and before completing the necessary assessment period there. This action on her part led to her son being placed with a foster carer. Although she had made changes to her lifestyle Jean could be very emotionally reactive and aggressive at times and frequently alienated the professionals involved in her case. After being homeless for a short time following her premature departure from the mother and baby unit, she managed to obtain her own accommodation and created some stability in her life. During an assessment undertaken by a clinical psychologist (as part of the legal proceedings) Jean disclosed she had been raped by a stranger when she was 13 years old. The psychological assessment indicated that while Jean could be difficult to engage she may benefit from therapeutic intervention that addressed the rape, the significant adversity in her background, and her challenging behaviour.

Summary of sessions

Jean had experienced significant rejection and maltreatment while in the care of her birth family. Unfortunately her experience of local authority care seemed to simply replace one form of adversity for another as instability, disruption and trauma characterised her adolescence and young adulthood. She had spent a significant period in an adolescent psychiatric unit leaving many of the professionals involved in the case questioning her mental health. Despite the adversity in her life she appeared to have some understanding of the impact these experiences had had on her and the need to change herself as well as her lifestyle. Becoming pregnant was a shock for her but proved to be a pivotal time in her life. She was described in the psychologist's assessment as having an 'anti-social, narcissistic personality style' which causes her to be somewhat 'distant, mistrustful and suspicious of others'. However, he also considered her to have potential despite her background.

In the early sessions with her she could react in an abusive, hostile fashion especially if she perceived she was (unfairly) criticised. She was especially reactive when someone disagreed with her, or pushed her on 'personal matters'; dealing with 'embarrassment' or 'shame' was likely to provoke an unnecessary and disproportionate response from her. In my early contact with her I could understand how she could be perceived by others as 'aggressive' and/or 'intimidating'. Many of the professionals including her social worker struggled to relate to her in a way that did not provoke further anger in her. She seemed comfortable when other people either retreated from the hostility or responded to her in a similar manner. Although many people, especially statutory professionals, experienced her in this way she had also developed some positive relationships; notably her solicitor, the foster carer, and the contact workers who supervised the contact with her son.

Recognising she could be selectively relational with some of the people involved in her life was a key element for me in the assessment. We struggled early on to engage when she was still at the mother and baby unit but that changed significantly once she had her own property. I later discovered that being at the unit reminded her of unhappy experiences in residential care and the psychiatric unit. By this stage she was fighting to have her son returned to her care. She was more relaxed in her own home and also less defensive; she was motivated and by this stage more easily engaged. She was beginning to understand the issues preventing her son's return to her care more clearly. One of the key tasks was helping her to realise that the angry, defensive way of coping was a fundamental problem and one of the obstacles to being reunited with her son. It not only alienated the professionals she needed to impress but also hindered the natural development of a support system that was an important prerequisite to reunification. For Jean it became a choice of losing the angry persona – or losing her baby son permanently – possibly to adoption. On the positive side she had developed good relationships with the support workers who supervised contact after a difficult early period. She also developed a remarkable relationship with the foster carer who she allowed to take something of a caring (therapeutic) role with her as well as her son.

When she had contact with her son she demonstrated her growing competence and confidence as a parent. Her affectionate overtures to him were reciprocated in warm interactions, which were increasingly observed by the professionals involved in the case. It became clear to me that Jean would not engage in therapy unless it was relevant to her in the 'here and now'. Dealing therapeutically with unresolved issues in her childhood in isolation from this would not have relevance for her. Part of making it relevant included dealing with the attachment issues arising out of their separation as a focus for the work. I knew this was a concern of hers as she feared her son's closeness to the foster carer replacing his relationship with her. It was also essential to help her relate more effectively to the professionals as well as those who may potentially form part of her support network in the future.

Previous assessments had indicated the need for her to address fundamental issues of 'anger management' in her lifestyle. Although she agreed to undertake this work with me she was initially suspicious as if I was going to 'mess with my head'. She found it helpful and became more interested when I discussed with her how this work had gone with other cases. Jean engaged well with this aspect and was able to relate to their experiences and later reflect on the meaning of it for her anger management. Discussing the problems of real people she could relate to made the approach more relevant for her.

Jean had been the victim and perpetrator of a great deal of violence and aggression in her life. As she reminded me, by virtue of her experience she was of course an expert on anger and getting angry. She quickly grasped the concept of 'anger management'; we were able to identify and understand: particular contexts for her; triggers leading to anger arousal; and the (physiological and psychological) detail of her own arousal pattern. After a few sessions she felt she could work out her own plan for dealing with her problem. She wanted to use the basic ideas we had discussed and make her own plan. I supported this as she seemed to understand by this time what was required of her. The plan had to be good enough (zero tolerance for violence) so that it was safe for her son to be returned to her care.

By this stage Jean had engaged well with me, and as a result of the anger management began relating more effectively to other professionals involved in the case. Jean was able to see results from this change of attitude fairly quickly making new relationships along the way. The following months saw something of a transformation in which she and the social worker developed a working relationship for the first time. This improved relationship between them allowed a more meaningful dialogue to take place in which the social worker could outline her concerns without Jean becoming angry and defensive. Eventually the social worker acknowledged the potential of reunification. Jean was concerned about the bond she had with her son weakening over time in favour of the close relationship she could see he had with the foster carer. Although she had a high regard for the foster carer she also feared he was closer to her and may not want to leave her. In sessions with her alone and at times with her son, we addressed the issue of maintaining their relationship together despite their enforced separation. This was supported by the contact workers as well as the foster carer who frequently talked of his mother to him – keeping the idea of her alive in his mind between the contact sessions. This approach enhanced the relationship Jean had with the foster carer, enabling her to feel more secure.

By this stage Jean had formed a relationship with a young man who after several months became her partner. I met him many times and observed him with the family during this time. He demonstrated a lot of commitment to them both and appeared very caring and supportive. During the therapy we had talked about 'picking a good one' as many of her previous relationships had been short-term, and often abusive and violent. Jean was so happy with him and struggled to accept that someone like this could want to be in a relationship with her. This was one of several turning points for her.

Once the social worker felt she could work with Jean and the relationship between her and her new partner looked very supportive, she changed from being resistant to reunification to accepting it. From this point the process of returning the child to the mother's care happened more quickly than I would have preferred. My involvement ceased just at the point of being reunited. I was concerned that there was a very limited support package provided for them, leaving the family still very vulnerable.

The research interview

Jean now lived in very comfortable rented accommodation with the same partner and two children. They'd had a child of their own since I last saw them and were pleased to show me how well they were doing as a family. Recalling the early period of my involvement Jean said 'I would shout at you for nothing . . . You would ask a question and I'd be off – I would do it with anyone.'

'In the beginning when I met you I wasn't happy . . . People couldn't get through to me no matter what they said . . . I was yo-yoing – then I would be alright for a time . . . I lost my temper with everyone.'

'I'd push everyone away – I didn't trust anyone'. She had an aggressive avoidant attachment style with most people.

She agreed it was a turning point when she discovered she was pregnant and made immediate changes to her lifestyle – giving up drugs, etc.

She recalled losing her son to care: 'John taken from me – broke my heart'. 'I loved him so much, I was an idiot'.

'After he was taken the next day – I did not know where he was; I didn't see him for three weeks'.

She recalled another turning point when the contact centre staff related better to her as she impressed them by the way she cared for John. She said:

'The staff made it difficult for me at first – patronising me, treating me like an idiot'. 'Something changed, I learned to trust them'. 'It took a while and they trusted me'.

'I've done everything they asked of me'. 'It was the happiest day of my life when he came home to me on his first birthday'.

'You won't beat the system they have more power'. I did everything they asked of me and now I'm here with my two kids'.

'I always trusted William' (Solicitor). He had been her solicitor since her time in juvenile court. He was her only trusting relationship for a long time until her current partner.

'I realised after two–three sessions with you, there was nothing to be scared of'. 'I'd get better each time'. 'After a while things changed in my head – anger management clicked'. 'You realise you are better off not losing your temper'.

'I started to feel scared and anxious when I did not lose my temper – like everyone else'. I knew I couldn't hit her even when she hit me' (referring to a confrontation with another young woman who had previously been a rival).

We talked about her experience with the social worker who was the same one throughout her case. Initially the social worker was against any reunification and suggested adoption in the care plan. 'She could see how hard I was trying'. 'It changed'. 'I realised she wasn't as bad as I thought – we get on well now'.

'I grew up a bit'.

Responding to the question on 'change' she acknowledged she became a different person when she lost the angry persona. She attributes most of the change influence to her partner, as well as the foster carer perhaps not acknowledging how much she influenced matters herself.

'The biggest change in my life was 'picking a good one' – referring to her partner. She says this openly in front of him to his embarrassment.

'I never thought I could settle down with someone. Every man I knew before was a total wanker; all men were the same in my eyes'.

'I had changed before but Andrew (partner) made a massive difference'. Before that time I did not want to be in a room with you or any man'. 'Normally I am nervous but for some reason it was OK'.

'He was funny and made me relaxed. He is brilliant with my son – he took me to contact'. 'I never want to be with another bloke even though I moan and shout at him sometimes. I remember thinking I hope he is not like the rest'.

Jean told me she is still in touch with the foster carers who cared for John. 'They did a good job – they really loved him'. 'I was worried he would love them and forget me. When I met them they were great and I could see they wanted me and John to be together'. I suggested she learned to trust them as well and she agreed.

'Its hard work with Social Services, I wish they understood better'. Jean reflected on the early stages of trying to convince them she could care for John. 'You have to realise you cannot beat the system – they have more power than you'.

Social Services were very pleased with developments and are planning to revoke the care order. We reflected on the progress made in three years since she discovered she was pregnant and how different her life could have been. Jean was very proud of her family and more mature and settled than I expected given her very difficult background. As a family they have continued to make progress. As an individual and as a mother Jean has learned to be more reflective and to understand herself. She has learned to trust appropriately and build close personal relationships that have become the cornerstone of her life.

Part III

Findings and discussion

Chapter 5

A working framework

'No chance, some chance, every chance' of engagement in therapy and successful rehabilitation

'Psychotherapy isn't what you think'.

(Bugental, 1999)

Overview

'Early work and engagement' is seen here as the essential key that helps you gain entry to the family's world, potentially laying the basis for all that may follow. Once entry has been gained and the nature and extent of the defensiveness is understood the assessment begins to take shape. The 'dimensions of therapeutic engagement' is not a formula but serves to help conceptualise and guide the assessment activity. Cases will vary considerably; to use a sporting metaphor: you must play what is in front of you.

As you engage this process you become aware of the role and the impact of parents' defensiveness in the unfolding dynamic. This phenomenon is defined here as 'Parents' response to professional intervention' having various presentations determined by historical factors influential in the parents' lives.

Next the reader is guided through the complexity of 'Parenting and parenting characteristics' where essential elements help define the parents' potential for personal growth. Finally, formulating the assessment provides a framework that gives shape and coherency to the massive amount of information gathered by you and others. Ultimately it provides your opinion ('no chance; some chance; every chance') on the future direction of the case and the prospects for the family; in particular the potential for the family engaging with therapy and being rehabilitated.

Introduction

The significance of 'early work and engagement', in this context as referred to throughout this book, cannot be overestimated. Although very much a challenge in its own right once established, it provides the essential foundation upon which everything else is built. The framework described here is not an alternative to other assessments, notably social work and child protection; psychology or psychiatry; or individual child assessment. It is something separate from them with distinct, specific areas of its own – but in many respects it naturally overlaps with other assessments in key areas. The framework acknowledges the complex, multidimensional aspect to the work. Its purpose is to focus on the internal and external relational world of the family, and in particular that of the parents – which is seen as pivotal to the well-being of the family. Ultimately it aims to provide assessments and intervention that enhance the prospects and well-being of children who are already disadvantaged by the experience of maltreatment, separation and disruption in their lives.

This is seen in the wider context of a 'risk aversive culture' and the influence it has on professional and parental activity. It aims to illuminate: a) functional and systemic problems affecting parenting and its impact on the well-being of the children in particular; and b) creative possibilities for what often amounts to fundamental change on the part of the parents. It seeks, wherever there is some hope for change ('some chance'), to create a context whereby professionals and parents can be appropriately relational with each other – so that even in the face of many obstacles and potential conflict – a 'meaningful conversation' can take place. It promotes the notion of professionals – whatever their discipline – 'being therapeutic' in the approach to engaging or supporting parents who often (in this formal context at least) start from a position of relational disadvantage. The framework is a closely linked companion to the multidimensional 'therapeutic approach' that is referred to in Chapter 8, and together guide assessment, as well as intervention wherever that may be possible.

This framework pays close attention to the part played by 'context' on the lives of the families – including to what extent they may be marginalised and feeling alienated by professional activity. The relationship between the professional system and the family is also a key component in the assessment. The framework aims to support the various professionals whose task it is to provide key assessments in these cases, in particular the Expert assessor considering therapeutic intervention in these complex cases – where thus far, obstacles to progress have stubbornly endured, despite everyone's best efforts.

The framework is presented here in four parts:

- Dimensions of therapeutic engagement
- Parents' response to professional intervention
- Parenting and parental characteristics
- Formulating the assessment

Dimensions of therapeutic engagement

Although there are psychometric tests that help identify some of the aspects referred to below this is essentially a relational exercise and assessment. I am aware that someone from a different modality and background could have identified quite different elements and/or a different format. In my reflections I have taken a wider perspective and tried not to be constrained by modality itself or other potential restrictions. To help unpick the complexity and meet the challenge of the multidimensional nature of this work I have searched (within myself and within the field of psychotherapy) extensively for ideas, tools and inspiration. Some of the elements identified will include familiar concepts that have been adapted so that their application has relevance and value in this context, and as a part of the overall framework.

The following aspects of psychological functioning and qualities of social relatedness have proven to be essential elements in uncovering parents' potential for therapeutic work and rehabilitation.

i) Willingness to engage
ii) Insight and ability to attach meaning to experience
iii) Willingness and ability to consider other perspectives
iv) Awareness of the need for change
v) Capacity for 'reflective functioning' and the ability to generate secure attachment experience
vi) Contextual factors and individual functioning

The purpose of the guideline is to establish the relevance and potential viability of therapeutic work in a particular case as well as identifying the pros and cons of specific areas of intervention. The following guidelines take as read, the need to appropriately involve the children at various points in the assessment. This is essential to accurately identify relationship factors, including attachment issues, but also particular characteristics of the child, which are often influential in the outcome. Child–parent closeness, boundaries, as well as the potential for family cohesiveness, and the work that needs to be undertaken with the child, must therefore involve the child. How you decide to do this will be determined by the vagaries of the case as well as your preferred methodology. Parents' potential for committing to the sessions (and the therapeutic process) is more easily gauged over several, rather than a single session, especially where there appears to be some potential.

i) Willingness to engage

Two factors are important here:

PARENT'S MOTIVATION

An individual or couple's motivation to commit to therapy/counselling is sometimes clearly evident from the outset, one way or the other. Other cases are less clear and benefit from being tested over several sessions in which core issues can be firstly explored and then closely examined to reveal more accurately what parents think and feel. In particular their motivation will be tested alongside their willingness to engage with sensitive and uncomfortable matters at the core of the case. Unfortunately, many parents are angry and extremely defensive and unable to engage despite your best efforts. Their motivation is to remain staunchly defensive and engage you in supporting their cause if possible – with little prospect of change. Others may be uncertain or more positively motivated, depending on the unfolding dynamics, and in particular to what extent they feel they can engage with and trust the assessor.

ABILITY TO TRUST AND MAKE RELATIONSHIPS

The level at which they are able to trust and form relationships will be evident in how they respond to the encounter with you and the process of assessment. It is reasonable to expect a parent to be anxious, reticent and defensive to some extent, during the initial session; they have to assess you as you assess them and determine to what extent they feel they can both engage with and trust you. If they appear motivated simply because it is the last or only resort – then in some cases it may be a start – but will not be enough in itself; by this stage their motivation should be increasingly driven, not by defensiveness, but by a need to address the identified problems and professional concerns. If there is some degree of trust and engagement you may be able to reach some agreement on the nature of the problems and a discernible method of addressing them. It is important from the parents' perspective that the nature of the problems and the method of addressing them is presented in an understandable and meaningful way for them. This in itself is quite challenging in some cases.

ii) Insight and ability to attach meaning to experience

Although associated with psychotherapy for more than a century and a word commonly used among the caring professions, 'insight' is not clearly understood (Castonguay and Hill, 2012). Insight in this context is understood to be the acquisition of new understanding and recognised to be a vehicle for change and personal growth in counselling and psychotherapy. It assumes a person has problems emanating from a lack of awareness and self-understanding preventing the development of more adaptive responses and behaviours. There is still much to discover regarding important clinical issues such as the link between insight and action on the part of the parent, and the therapist–client role in generating insight experience.

Assessing an individual's level of insight is not straightforward or easily quantifiable. A great deal depends on the engagement and the quality of interaction with the family. The assessor will be seeking to assess a parent's capacity for insight, including their potential in this regard, on a continuum with a range from being: generally not reflective and insightful, to some capacity and/or potential to understand their own behaviour and problems, to having a good capacity to understand their own and others' mental processes. Insight in this context can, via a therapeutic encounter, help a parent reflect, understand and then progress to attaching meaning to past behaviours and/or experiences in a way that was not previously available to them. If acquired in this way a parent can develop the potential for anticipating problems that previously overwhelmed them and change their future responses and behaviours. Progress in this area, in combination with other factors can lead to potentially transformative change.

iii) Willingness and ability to consider other perspectives

Parents who successfully navigate legal proceedings have been able to do so because they have both recognised the need, as well as (in part at least) developed and utilised the skills, to negotiate with professionals. They may have started some way from this eventual position but learned to accept that there are often several other perspectives taken by others, regarding their behaviour and the core issues in the case. They learn that in order to progress their case it is essential to take account of this, uncomfortable and even painful though this may be for them at times. Some parents learn this and adapt earlier. Others fail to see the relevance of considering alternative perspectives they perceive as wrong or untrue, and know only how to fight their corner. Engaging with professionals and discussing various perspectives, they will perceive as the domain of the professionals, and may therefore feel less comfortable and even vulnerable. In some cases parents have been able to move from a position of implacable resistance to a perspective other than their own, to a more open position where at least the other perspectives are considered and can be part of a debate. Parents, in these cases, often have to contend with, what for them amounts to overwhelming feelings of anger, frustration, and growing resentment when challenged by the different perspectives of others. However, sometimes against the odds, whether initiated by the parents, or assisted by a professional, a change in their attitude, when it happens, can have a profound impact on the nature of parental motivation and involvement in the case. In doing so, they move closer to rejecting their original position of implacable resistance to whatever others may think and feel; a position that has led to conflict, alienation and polarised positions.

The nature of complex, adversarial childcare legal proceedings is that fixed positions can be taken and defended by parents as well as some professionals. In these circumstances parents can fail to develop and/or maintain relationships with professionals as they become occupied completely with defending their case. An ability to understand and to some extent take account of other perspectives, even when passionately disagreeing with them, can help the parents take a more balanced view of proceedings and assist in a continuing dialogue with those who were previously their antagonists. The ability to consider other perspectives in this way may also reflect a certain mental flexibility on their part that may be of benefit if therapeutic work is recommended.

iv) Awareness of the need for change

This is a close first cousin to the previous quality. Some parents will utterly reject the need for change, externalising responsibilities and largely blaming others for events and concerns that have been identified by the authorities. Other parents will have less of a fixed position, which becomes more evident if you can engage them in a positive way. When we talk about change it is usually at a variety of levels and in differing contexts including: self-understanding and personal growth; behavioural change; family functioning and/or lifestyle change (e.g. substance misuse); relational change; change that acknowledges culpability and responsibility for key events. It is also often at a level whereby the authorities and the court, perceive change to have taken place based on their observation and/or experience of the parents. Sometimes the need for change begins somewhat grudgingly and is limited to a specific area and a given set of circumstances. Judgement will have to be exercised to ascertain whether at this stage it may be the beginning of more profound developments or the actual limit of their potential. This process is assisted by taking a non-judgemental approach and, as much as possible, avoiding the use of pejorative narrative with the parents. You will not be the first person speaking with the parents about these sensitive matters and you will want to avoid the pattern of previous encounters with statutory professionals, if they have been negative. Avoiding pejorative narrative and being non-judgemental in approach can contribute toward a different experience for parents, generating a less defensive response in some cases. From the parents' perspective, when they are positively engaged in this way for the first time, it can sometimes feel like exploring familiar issues in a new way.

The awareness of the need for change at various levels on the part of parents is perceived to extend on a continuum from:

- No awareness, including implacable resistance, to
- Some awareness, but also fluctuating resistance, to
- Developed awareness, with little to no resistance and acceptance of the need for help.

Either ends of the continuum are more easily defined; it is the middle group that will challenge the assessment of their potential. It is also difficult if they are only able to relate to you (and no other professional), about their feelings and the need for change – though this may be an important first stage. Coming to a view about some parents' potential is a challenge and in some cases requires more than one session in order to define their potential.

v) Capacity for 'reflective functioning' and ability to generate secure attachment experience

Reflective functioning refers to the essential human capacity to understand behaviour in light of underlying mental states and intentions. The construct, introduced by Fonaghy *et al.* in 1991, in this context refers to the parents' capacity to hold the child's mental state in mind and in a routine way determines the quality of interaction in any parental response to the child. In a similar way, assessing a parent's potential to generate secure attachments can be observed by the way parents respond to their infants' needs in terms of: availability, sensitivity, reliability, responsiveness and predictability. The qualities engendered in reflective functioning and generating secure attachment experiences are closely linked. Together they combine to form the basis for developing positive, resilient relationships between the child and caregiver, enhancing the child's developmental prospects in the process. This part of the assessment must involve seeing the children and parents together. However, it invariably needs a discussion with parents separately as well, to access their perceptions and reasoning in relation to the children's needs and behaviours, and their responses to that.

During the contact session, rather than just observe the interaction in the family, I often become involved with them to see if I can establish more clearly the parents' motivation and thinking in relation to the parent–child activity. This helps me to have a considered view about the child and their needs and to what extent the parent has awareness of this and can adapt to meet the requirements. In this way I can also see if there is potential to trigger new thoughts, ideas and understanding on the part of the parent and/or if this might be the substance of the therapeutic work at another time. I very much like to mix and match individual child, couple and family sessions in order to explore the potential and identify possible obstacles to progress. In this way you are viewing the family difficulties from several perspectives offering a window on the family's relational world, including the obstacles to progress as well as potential for growth. It will also illuminate the parents' defensive inclinations and to what extent they can overcome these difficulties and focus on the sensitive area of parent–child behaviour and relationships. Explorations in this area will often provide the strongest indication of the parents' potential for therapeutic work and rehabilitation.

vi) Contextual factors and individual functioning

This refers to how various factors potentially influence the parents' functioning in relation to their child as well as their potential to engage with therapy and support. For example this may include the parents': mental health; substance misuse; personality disorder; domestic violence or unsafe-partner relationships, etc.

This does not refer directly to assessing whether a parent has a personality disorder, or a psychological or psychiatric state, or the extent of their substance misuse. As a psychotherapist, these are issues that will have been assessed by others. In such cases there is still a critical need to assess the extent, and in what circumstances, these factors may affect a parent's capacity to: undertake the parenting role, be consistently and appropriately relational to meet the emotional needs of the child, engage in therapy; as well as what criteria you may set for working with the parents: for example, drug free, zero tolerance for physical violence, and to what extent they might benefit from any support and/or therapeutic intervention. While some recommendations may have already been made by another Expert in this regard, unless there are clear indications not to do so, it is still important to assess from a psychotherapy perspective, the parents' ability to engage in a meaningful way, but taking account of the influence of one or combinations of the above factors. In this regard having one or more of the above does not necessarily exclude parents from a favourable assessment or further work – but they are frequently important, influential factors that will be very relevant to the outcome of the assessment.

Parents' response to professional intervention

Parents' reaction to serious professional concerns regarding the care of their child is one of the factors that will often determine whether children are removed, legal proceedings are initiated, and/or help and support is provided to the family. Being able to consider the professionals concerns and work with them in a positive fashion is often critical to the outcome, and is frequently a pivotal point in the whole process. As already referred to, this process often does not work smoothly as it is challenged by complexity, conflict between parents and professionals, and a failure to work together. Many parents in this position will naturally feel stressed and react defensively to the perceived threat – triggered by intense feelings of shame that can inhibit or undermine the critical early relationship activity between the parent and social worker (Kavner and McNab, 2005; Flaskas, 1997). Parents' defensive behaviour in this context, is conceptualised here as an organised strategy to deal with not only the current (unconscious) threat to the 'self' – but the imminent threat to the integrity and viability of the family. The threat to 'self' and the subsequent defensive response is likely to be an established pattern that has its source in much earlier unresolved (attachment) experience (Kennedy, 2005).

It is therefore important to understand the parents' defensiveness in terms of their underlying mental state, – especially their level of emotional and psychological distress – that is the motivation for their response. It is naturally experienced by professionals on the receiving end of this behaviour as 'resistance' and sometimes seen pejoratively, as reflecting negative aspects of the parents' personality, and likely to prevent any progress.

The variations

ANGRY-DEFENSIVE

In this category the parent feels deeply threatened by an impending sense of shame triggered by professional (often child protection) involvement. In order to protect the 'self', the parent unconsciously externalises the threat via an angry/defensive response that tends to distance or push away the professional they need to engage with. Often the parent will be so engrossed in the defensiveness she/he will be unaware of the effect their response has had on the professional. This early failure to understand each other's respective positions and responses is critical to the outcome. As a result of this failed early engagement it is likely that little if any 'meaningful conversation' has taken place between them. The severity and extent of the parent's angry defence, and the professional's response, will largely determine how widespread the disagreement is on many issues as well as potentially laying down the basis for ongoing conflict. Where the conflict becomes intense, issues and differences of opinion can easily become personalised and positions can become ever more polarised.

Parents here may see professionals as at least partially (sometimes wholly) to blame for the circumstances and commonly voice such perceptions – 'they did nothing to help' or 'they wanted the children away from us whatever we did'. Often their energy is wholly committed in response to the perceived threat and their survival as a family. They may see no alternative to this way of being – which they may feel prevents their humiliation and at the same time maintains some credibility for themselves. This inherently stressful position with its narrow, defensive outlook, has little scope to consider other perspectives, or to reflect more meaningfully on the nature of their difficulties – whether it be with their children, as parents, or with the professionals involved in their case. The professionals can sometimes experience these parents as threatening, unnecessarily resistant, disrespectful, and 'not working with the department'. Often parents in this category seem unable to reflect and have little to no narrative that offers a rationale for their circumstances beyond blaming others, especially the professionals. Some parents may be utterly committed to defensive engagements of this nature whatever the intervention, and are clearly beyond the scope of therapeutic intervention. Others, when they are engaged can be coaxed to reflect a little and consider alternative perspectives, without constantly resorting to externalising responsibility and blame toward others and distancing those who may be able to help. Progress or otherwise will hinge on their potential in this regard.

AMBIVALENT

In response to the stress of the child protection investigation and professional involvement these parents commonly oscillate between positions of being angry/defensive and dependent. Their anger is not as severe as the previous category and tends to be more internalised. They are extremely anxious, even fearful of the consequences, and unable to relate in a consistent fashion and form a stable relationship with the social worker. Their affective response will be dependent on the nature of the stress, to what extent they feel held or supported, and what kind of behaviour they perceive will bring the desired professional response – at a given point in time. The parents' ambivalence effectively deflects pressure from them toward the professional they are engaged with who may not completely understand the impact of this dynamic on them.

This type of parental response is difficult for social workers to deal with as it generates feelings of uncertainty, being overly responsible, or frustration and sometimes anger with the parent in this context. This can be very challenging for the social worker who on the one hand has to contend with feelings of parental anger, while at the same time being made to feel guilty or overly responsible for their well-being. The nature of this kind of ambivalence wears away at the potential relationship base between the professional and the parent. Understanding this as a relational pattern motivated by severe anxiety on the part of the parent is the first stage in making progress with this dynamic.

The mother in the Smith family (Case Study 1) was an example of this in the early stages of the casework. Engaging with her was challenging as you felt the 'push and the pull' of the way she related – often manipulating people and circumstances as she sought to protect herself from criticism and feelings of guilt and shame. Taking a direct approach to this kind of problem, challenging the mother, would simply incur stronger resistance. Change was brought about by engaging in the relationship – based on an understanding of the nature of the dynamic, and its role in protecting the mother's sense of 'self' in particular. These sensitive matters could only be explored in the context of a trusting, therapeutic relationship over a period of time. The mother showed herself to be adaptable to a tolerant, less confrontational approach that conveyed an interest in her well-being.

CONTRITE – ACQUIESCENT

Essentially these are parents who present as being very sorry for the actions that led to their children's removal and want to do all they can to make it right. They may initially have been angry/aggressive in their presentation but have significantly shifted their response. The biggest change is that they now appear to accept culpability and responsibility for what happened after initially presenting as resistant and defensive. The salutary experience of having their children removed from their care and the potential finality of legal proceedings, as well as many other potential factors, has a profound effect on some parents. One parent described this as an 'epiphany' – a life-changing experience.

Naturally being contrite at this late stage is not sufficient in itself to change matters and would not prevent a careful examination of the circumstances, including parents' functioning. Often these parents, as they become increasingly aware of their responsibility for their circumstances, experience guilt – with many feeling anxious and/or depressed. These are feelings that potentially undermine, even incapacitate some parents' efforts to regain a position of authority and credibility with their children, as well as with the professionals. Sometimes parents in this position want others to determine what they should do – fearful their own action or initiative will lead to failure. Sudden, and what appear to be quite profound, changes in parents' attitude and behaviours is unfortunately not always sustained. Though there are notable exceptions that, when provided with support, result in transformative change.

The father in the Morris family (Case Study 3) is an example of someone profoundly influenced by an 'epiphany' – a truly life-changing experience, the consequences of which were still with him three years later when I met him for the research interview. He became highly motivated as a result of the experience (the loss of his children to foster care), and significantly changed his lifestyle, attitude and approach to professionals, and was successfully rehabilitated with his wife and four children.

UNASSERTIVE (OVERWHELMED) – DEPENDENT

This response often (but not exclusively) applies to single parents (young single mothers in my study) who have had very unsatisfactory relationships, involving domestic violence, substance misuse, or dominant exploitative partners who have been a threat to the children. Some will have experienced a series of such relationships with negative consequences for themselves as well as their children. They may be superficially socially skilled but have little to no internal frame of reference to guide their parenting, or any relationship activity – so trust, intimacy and friendship-building has often become a superficial and therefore very risky process. Often these parents seem oblivious to the consequences of such rapid relationship changes in their lives; particularly with changing roles – as acquaintances become friends, become partners, then step-parents – sometimes in a remarkably short space of time. These parents have a pattern of becoming quickly but superficially attached and dependent on new partners who may initially appear helpful to them. They may also be anxious, lacking self-confidence and completely unable to deal with authority figures in their lives – either informally (partners) or formally (social worker, etc.). For some of these parents the patterns are well established and not subject to change in the timescale for the child. However, there is a relatively small proportion of parents who, despite considerable difficulties, will have an awareness of their vulnerability and even some insight into the processes that have led to such disastrous outcomes for them and their children – though as yet they can foresee no alternative to this way of being. They may even be indicating a general commitment to change – but have little to no idea how to achieve that. In these cases the therapy may start from a position of some dependency on the part of the parent; as trust and confidence gradually develop they can be helped to understand and then change patterns of relational dependency in their lives, especially with unsuitable partners who represent the most serious concerns for the children's safety and well-being. Helping the parents develop a relationship frame to guide their future activity is important here especially as far as close personal relationships (their children and partner or potential partner) are concerned. Developing and sustaining appropriate personal relationships that are stable, while maintaining safe patterns for family life – is the (therapeutic) challenge in working with these parents.

There is a good example of this category in the Knight family (Case Study 4). Here the mother had her three children removed from her care after a period of several, very unsafe, partner-relationships that jeopardised the well-being of the children as well as the mother. She had been completely dominated by the partners she had allowed into the home after knowing them only a few days. Initially she presented as overwhelmed and dependent with very little potential for change. However, over the time of the legal proceedings, she gradually engaged with the professionals. Slowly her personality began to emerge and although still lacking self-confidence she began responding to interventions and demonstrated previously unseen levels of resilience. Recognising the mother had some potential relatively early in the process offered her the (therapeutic) opportunity for overcoming the considerable obstacles to being rehabilitated with her three children, who would otherwise have been placed for adoption. The rehabilitation took almost a year but was founded on the early assessment that the mother may have some potential.

Parenting and parental characteristics

The assessment focuses on five main parameters which refer to parental characteristics and aspects of their functioning: A) Skills/techniques; B) Parents' developmental knowledge; C) Social relatedness/parent to child; D) Cognitive/psychological ability; E) Sense of self.

'These parameters are influential individually and collectively in the way parents relate especially: with their partner; to the children; with key professionals; and then potentially in a therapeutic relationship. At the core is the parents' capacity (current as well as potential) to be empathic and 'attuned' to the needs of the child and to be sufficiently relational to generate a secure attachment experience. Here the assessment focuses on subtle interactions that draw heavily across the domains of parental functioning including the parent themselves and their innate qualities. The child is naturally a player in this – their characteristics, their resilience or vulnerability, and their potential to recover from the consequences of maltreatment and separation; their motivation and potential to reconnect to the parent in the timescale, are also critical to the outcome. The assessment will not just identify the existence or otherwise of these characteristics but assess the quality, the potential for growth, and what obstacles (if any) prevent their development. Also what support and/or therapy is required to enhance their prospects.

The assessment framework relies on a close examination and subsequent analysis of the data as it relates to the parameters described in this section. Although the parameters are described separately it is essential to understand the connections and subtle interrelationship between each of them. For example for a parent to undertake a childcare task successfully they often need to draw on a range of aptitudes including; knowledge about the child and/or child development, cognitive ability to organise and/or problem-solve; an ability to engage and relate with a child to obtain compliance, etc. The more demanding the task the more heavily it draws from each of the domains including the parent's personal resources such as resilience, motivation and other qualities embedded in an individual's 'sense of self'. The 'self' in this regard is considered to not only help manage the interrelationship between each of the parameters but enables social responses to be appropriate, consistent and coherent (See Figure 5.1).

Assessment of the parameters and subsequent analysis can indicate the parent's capacity for therapeutic intervention and potential rehabilitation. As a result, it is possible to describe to other professionals where on the continuum the parent's current level of functioning is estimated to be, as well as their potential for growth and personal development. It is possible to identify factors that will be influential in this process in addition to therapy, such as support; psycho-educational input; improved or reduced family contact, etc. It will also identify factors likely to hinder progress and be harmful to the child, for example, factors that disrupt or undermine the stability of the child's placement.

Ultimately the framework will help to identify parents on a continuum in terms of their capacity, or potential capacity for engaging in therapy that will lead to rehabilitation with their children. This is described on the continuum as: 'every chance, some chance, or no chance' of benefitting from therapeutic work leading to rehabilitation. Factors that may influence the case either way will also be identified and developed in the assessment. The recommendations in the assessment will naturally be constrained by factors such as: timescale for the child; availability of financial resources; and interventions dependent on specific (often unavailable) expertise.

Although this assessment particularly focuses on the parents' 'sense of self', and their ability to relate, it considers all the parameters described in this assessment to be relevant and influential. The following is a description of each of the parameters in this framework and their interrelationship.

A) Skills/techniques

This parameter refers to the skills/techniques relevant to the role of parenting such as: general childcare, age appropriate child management skill; domestic skills; organising skills for family life, etc. Other skills such as assertiveness training or anger management are also often identified as relevant interventions for one or both parents in many cases. Where parenting is deemed 'not good enough' parental deficits are often identified in terms of parenting and associated skills. The solution is often seen as parents, if they are sufficiently motivated, working to acquire the necessary skills to raise them to a level that is 'good enough'. It is rarely that straightforward in complex cases that have travelled this far in legal proceedings. When skills-based intervention is provided for the parents and fails to produce the necessary results it is perceived to reflect negatively on them and their motivation. Their basic incompetence as parents is confirmed, defining their status as 'not good enough' parents ('no chance') with little prospect of realistic change occurring in the timescale for the child. At this stage of the assessment it is worth considering whether any intervention that was provided for them and considered to be unsuccessful, was timely, appropriate, and of sufficient quality to address the level and complexity of need.

For example I have had experience of parents who failed to make significant changes to their parenting via a general group work approach to parent-skills training but who later responded very well to an individually tailored approach provided by myself and a colleague. The parents were unhappy attending a group and felt they had been coerced into attending as it was the only intervention available. The group approach to providing general parenting skills is of great benefit to many parents experiencing problems in their child care. However, it was too general in its approach and had little relevance in this case; it had neither the quality nor the specific focus required to address the parents' complex needs. The individual approach was able to sensitively address therapeutic issues that naturally arose in the course of the intervention.

This was very much the case with the Bevan family (Case Study 2) where the mother had mental health difficulties and a history of sexual abuse as a child; she was unable to cope in a group setting. She was very anxious and feared her abuse, and other sensitive circumstances, being exposed in front of the other parents. She was aware of the need for assistance with parenting skills but because her son had ADHD and other developmental problems, she understood that a more specific programme would benefit them. Although not wanting to directly address the sexual abuse at the outset she gradually acquiesced as the need to do so arose several times in the context of individual-based parenting skills.

It is important to establish whether parents have an aptitude for learning and integrating new skills ('Doing stuff') and what will help facilitate that for them. In some cases identifying skills deficits is less of a problem than understanding the relationship between this and other aspects of their functioning, and providing an appropriate intervention specific enough to meet their needs. This kind of assessment very much requires expertise in this therapeutic preparation area and can often inform what other professionals do or don't do in respect of viable and appropriate interventions. However, it is an unfortunate reality that there is a dearth of resources in many areas that provide the expertise as well as the range and level of intervention necessary to help these families.

In terms of skills, being able to multitask is an important parenting capability, which draws heavily on the other parameters. Parents who demonstrate this quality often have an innate ability that may compensate for the lack of the same skill in their partner. Therefore in some cases assessing what the parents potentially bring collectively as a skill set will be relevant.

B) Parents' developmental knowledge

Most parents, while having some knowledge of children, and child development, and in general terms knowing how to be a parent before the arrival of their first child – mostly learn on the job. By integrating a variety of experiences, including caring for the child, the basis for a developing parenting model is laid. This in turn determines the nature and quality of parental activity with the child and is further shaped by ongoing experience. Parental knowledge and resulting beliefs therefore are at the core of parental activity. It is influential at many levels including basic parenting competence, as well as in their relationship to the role of parenting (Reder and Lucey, 1995). New information and knowledge as it is acquired via experience continues to shape the model, enabling very necessary modification to take place as the child's needs evolve with development and other changing circumstances. In this way parents naturally develop a knowledge base that potentially enables them to acquire a sense of competence, self-confidence, and positive self-identity in the role of parent. We know that parents' experience of being parented themselves is also relevant and can have a positive and negative influence here (Reder *et al.*, 2003). In some cases there may be specific issues relating to a particular child (e.g. child health issues; learning or physical disability; or mental health, etc.) where more than a rudimentary knowledge is required by parents so that they can make adjustments and appropriately meet the child's needs. This is often the case with children rehabilitated to their parents' care after an enforced separation; they will have been affected, sometimes quite profoundly by their experiences (pre-care as well as the separation and return), the challenge of which will raise the bar of parental competence to meet their needs.

This was the case with the Morris family (Case Study 3) who discovered that, despite making considerable improvements as parents, the children's needs had changed while away from their care. Now added to the mix, on their return to the family, were new attachment issues and behavioural difficulties. To combat this, parents will need to acquire knowledge and understanding of the impact the separation and other experiences have had on their children. Being able to empathise with the nature of the child's experiences and relating this to their presenting behaviour (attunement), plays a key role in meeting their needs.

In the course of assessment the extent of the parents' knowledge base and general understanding of the child's needs, and how this relates to their expectations of the child will become evident. Gaps and/or misunderstandings in their parental knowledge base can usefully be identified at this stage, forming the basis of an intervention, or as part of the therapeutic plan if there is potential for further work.

C) Social relatedness/parent to child

Parents' ability to relate well to their children and on behalf of the family within its social world, is an essential element in:

- Attachment and the relationship development with the child;
- Developing a social network to the family's benefit; and
- Providing appropriate links with the social world commensurate with the developmental needs of the child and family.

It is also an important factor in ensuring a parent's social and psychological well-being. An individual's personality characteristics and ability to socially relate will have many influences throughout their development. Children form social concepts, especially of themselves and of the people with whom they interact, in order to make sense of their experiences in interpersonal situations (Schaffer, 1998). Influential here is a child's attachment experience and its influence on the developing 'sense of self'. Many of the foundations for social relatedness are therefore formed early on, with the course of its development dependent on and highly influenced by the quality of social and other experiences along the way. Key in this development is an individual's understanding of the relationship between 'self' and 'other', their perception of the world, empathy, and the mental capacity to understand and relate to the motives and intentions of others.

In this part of the assessment attention is paid to the parents' capacity to be both generally and more specifically relational in their functioning. It is particularly concerned with the specific areas referred to earlier; that is, their ability to be appropriately relational with their children; their partner; key professionals involved; and in developing and maintaining a support network. Each of these areas needs to be considered as far as potential strengths and weaknesses are concerned as well as factors that may weaken or enhance their potential. Social relatedness refers to being ready-willing-able to understand/relate to the mental perspectives and emotional experience of others – especially to those within their family. If serious problems with social relatedness are identified they need to be defined in terms of potential for change – especially as it may impact on the parents' potential to be 'attuned' and to generate a secure attachment experience for their child.

In Case Study 5, Jean was a young single mother with a history of substance misuse who was angry and at times aggressive with others, including professionals. She was however, never angry with her baby and showed an impressive sensitivity in the care she provided for him. This was observed by the key professionals responsible for contact as well as myself. She had been drug free since she discovered she was pregnant and was able to generate secure attachment experiences for her child and seemed very able to relate to and understand (reflective functioning) how her child was experiencing the world. Her difficulty in social relatedness was more to do with an anger toward professionals (by whom she felt let down) and others who she perceived as a threat. She was not angry with everyone and demonstrated she could relate well at times with some professionals. The mother had some understanding of how she related to others and why – though was ambivalent and found it difficult to change. She had some insight as far as this phenomenon was concerned and was increasingly motivated to change in order to have her child returned to her care.

Professionals, in their assessment of the mother were influenced by the intensity of her anger at times. I saw the picture as somewhat mixed but was impressed with her ability to be sensitive to the needs of her child as well as an ability to relate quite well when not emotionally aroused or feeling threatened. She also demonstrated some insight and ability to reflect that I considered may be a basis for further work. Slowly and gradually she became more relational and eventually developed a good relationship with the social worker who had removed her child.

Assessing and defining the nature of a parent's problems with social relatedness may be key in some cases in deciding the potential for personal growth and therapeutic intervention. Of important consideration here are parents whose functioning may be affected by substance misuse, learning difficulties, mental health and personality disorder. These are important contextual factors that do not necessarily rule a parent out of consideration for further work and rehabilitation. There are often many contextual factors in the mix that need to be considered; though to what extent the assessment considers the parent has potential for personal growth will be the critical factor in the assessment.

D) Cognitive/psychological ability

This refers to mental activity and behaviour through which knowledge of the world is attained and processed, including learning, memory, thinking and problem-solving. Becoming a parenting is all about learning from new experiences, in a meaningful way, so that competence and confidence in the role grows. It is about assimilating considerable amounts of new information and integrating child-related experiences in a way that potentially enhances parent and child – as well as the developing relationship. Cognitive or psychological ability plays a significant role in enabling this process to take place; allowing information to be integrated, stored and called upon when required; facilitating problem-solving; organising and planning family life, etc. Specific deficits and other factors likely to affect this process are often identified in a psychological assessment, particularly global and specific learning difficulties and other functional (psychological) problems, such as personality disorders, that may be relevant. Whatever factors are identified need to be understood in terms of the limitations they may naturally impose on the quality and capacity for parenting, as well as their potential impact on the parents' ability to acquire – not just parenting skills – but the relational resources necessary to meet the developing needs of the child. Potential cognitive strengths as well as weaknesses can be identified. Unusually, two of the case studies (Case Study 1: the Smith family; and Case Study 3: the Morris family) referred to earlier, provide an example of a parent with superior intelligence – which in itself had a significant (positive and negative) bearing on the case. The mother in the Smith family used her considerable intelligence to build strategies that undermined professional activity and exacerbated conflict – thus avoiding confronting the shame and pain of parental culpability – a key therapeutic theme in the case. Understanding this phenomenon and delicately and gradually shifting the focus from a strategy of external conflict to one of internal exploration, was the key to change in this case.

E) Sense of self

'In each of us, the ensemble of body proper, brain, and mind interact to generate the relatively stable internal point of reference known as the self' (Wallin, 2007). An individual's 'sense of self' is seen as a cluster of beliefs and perceptions they have of themselves, especially regarding their various roles, associations, attributes, enduring patterns of emotional response and behaviour, and other important aspects that reflect their unique responses to experience. In the words of Allan Schore: 'The core of the self lies in patterns of affect regulation' (1994). Alongside our unique physical characteristics the uniqueness of self is what differentiates us from others. This is the part of a person that, either consciously or unconsciously, experiences life but also shapes it. Here, the 'sense of self' is seen as both the core and the glue holding all these elements together. It is also where we find an individual's particular personality characteristics, resilience to deal with stress, and motivation to remain committed to meet challenges as they arise – all of which are relevant in this context.

The relationship between 'sense of self' and other parameters, as well as the interrelationship between each of the parameters with each other, is also of fundamental importance. In this framework there is perceived to be a critical relationship between an individual's 'sense of self' and their ability to relate to those they are closest too. While highlighting potential areas for therapeutic intervention it will also help determine how effectively relational someone can be and therefore the prospects for them being able to engage in therapy. Any problems identified for therapeutic intervention must be considered in a timescale that is relevant for the child.

The relationship between 'sense of self' and other parameters in terms of their internal locus for change is also crucial; as is the extent the parent can understand and relate to the existence of internal as well as external influences on their thoughts, actions and behaviour. These considerations take us quite naturally into (tentatively) exploring with the parent the significance of change in the parent's internal and/or external world. Sometimes it becomes apparent that a similar level of understanding is also relevant for the professionals involved with the family, as well as between the parents and therapist. For example, it is often not sufficient for professionals – who want parents to change an aspect of their parenting or behaviour – to tell them they must change, or give instruction, advice and direct them to parenting classes because it is the only available intervention. The attempt at change has to be targeted in the right (internal or external) areas, it has to be timely, appropriate, meaningful and usable for the parents to have any chance of success.

Change in this regard is a far more sophisticated process that draws heavily across the parameters of not just 'Developmental knowledge' and 'Cognitive/ psychological', referred to earlier. It potentially crosses all parameters reaching deep into the resources contained in the self – where there may be historical (therapeutic) obstacles preventing progress that need attention. In the context of a therapeutic relationship it is possible to assess the potential for enhancing the parent's 'sense of self' and generating personal growth. Where this is possible the benefits are considerable. Where the 'self' can be used to reach across and engage the various domains in this way, any new learning is more likely to be integrated, become a part of them, and generalise to their day-to-day living experience. Parents will also feel motivated to use any new learning acquired in this way and potentially put their own creative stamp on it, increasing the chances of the learning being integrated, with the benefits 'generalising' to other contexts.

An example of this is in the Wilson case (5) where Jean, the young mother insisted on developing her own anger management plan after only two of the planned five sessions. She argued that she understood the principles, was an expert on violence and knew herself well enough by this stage and would be able to devise a suitable plan that would work for her. I knew she wanted to put her stamp on it and was motivated to succeed and went with her proposal, resulting in a very positive outcome. Encouraging and enhancing 'self' to play a part often represents the core of the therapeutic work.

When this level of change is generated in parents it can potentially transform the prospects for them and their families.

Summary

Having made the assessment, the worker will have an appreciation of the possibilities for therapeutic engagement, an understanding of the family's usual way of responding to professional involvement, and an outline of the parent characteristics that frame what they do with the child. A great deal is now known about the family's functioning in key areas, and its prospects for the future, which is of central importance to the assessment. However, there is still a great deal to do in order to bring shape and coherency to the assessment so that it is fit for purpose.

Formulating the assessment

Reaching conclusions

The huge amount of information accumulated from various sources including direct work places the professional with the challenge of extrapolating meaning and reaching conclusions regarding the issues of central importance in the case. For the court-appointed Expert this process is guided by the letter of instruction from the court whereas, for the general worker, professional principles will be determining the nature of the conclusions that are required. Importantly they will include: the needs of the child and the prospects for the parents being able to meet them in a timescale that is reasonable for the child; your interpretation of the key issues and the obstacles and prospects for change; and an analysis and interpretation of the process (family/legal/professional) that has brought

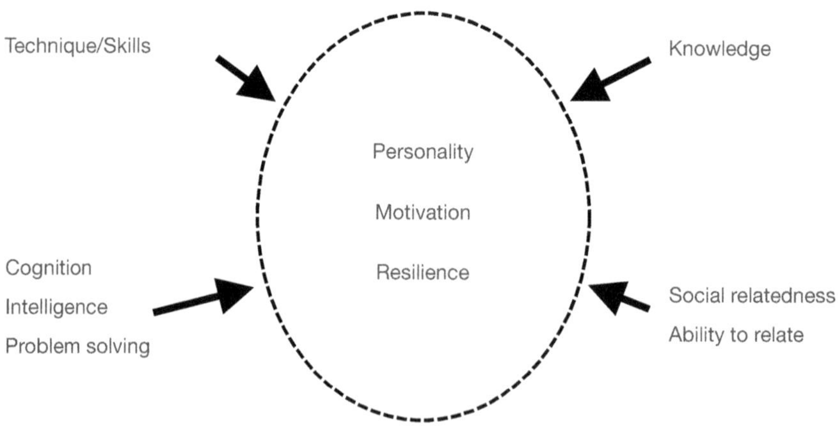

Figure 5.1 Assessment parameters and their interrelationships

us to this point. The family problems are likely to be complex and multifaceted with a significant history often dating back to the parents' childhood. It is essentially complex and there may be conflicting views regarding the interpretation of events, future direction, the prospects for the family, and the needs of the child. In my view the enormous amount of information provided to Experts is often a handicap rather than a help; however, there is a prevailing professional/legal view that you must have all the information in order to assess and understand the case.

The challenge is also to make it understood and meaningful for the family. Although this is often an organic process that grows out of the shared exploration with the family – that is (when possible) the assessment experience. Finally the assessment has of course to be presentable for the court and the professional system and able to withstand careful scrutiny and perhaps cross-examination.

One of the most difficult tasks is to extrapolate meaning and coherency from the enormous amount of detail available in your assessment in order to define a parent's potential in key areas that will in turn help determine the prospects for the family.

Defining parents' potential

Here the parents' potential to be rehabilitated with their children is defined on a continuum (see Figure 5.2) ranging from 'no chance' – to 'some chance' – to 'every chance' – with gradations along the way. Where parents are defined on the continuum will be attributable to a variety of potential factors as identified in the assessment by others as well as by you. Parents' position on the continuum is potentially fluid depending on their reactions to professional concerns and interventions, including the assessment. In relation to parents' position on the continuum it is also important to define the factors that may either weaken or enhance their prospects. For example: parental abstinence from substances and/or therapy to address the domestic violence. Some parents' prospects will shift along the continuum as family circumstances improve or deteriorate (e.g. fluctuations in a parent's mental state; severe periodic substance misuse; epiphany). Either way, this creates stress for the parents and potential instability for the children.

An influential factor in the assessment will be the extent to which the parents engaged and reached an understanding on the key issues of central importance in the case. The issues of central importance will include: the needs of the children which may have changed since their removal to foster care; the parents' sense of culpability and responsibility for the key events leading up to this point; and the ability to engage in therapy and other recommended interventions. The references to 'no chance; some chance; and every chance' should be understood in terms of a reasonable timescale for the child.

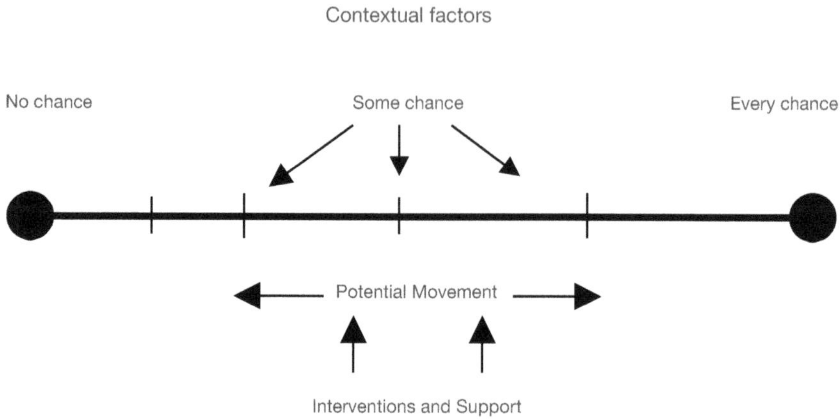

Figure 5.2 A continuum reflecting parents' potential to engage in therapy and be rehabilitated with their children

Defining 'no chance'

Here there are two sub-categories:

a) Fundamentally damaged with little potential for change; or
b) Very damaged with little capacity for change:

a) Parents in this category are likely to have significant deficits in most if not all areas. Most significantly, they will have a fundamentally damaged 'sense of self' also referred to as 'innate developmental damage' affecting functioning at all levels especially their ability to be generally and specifically relational. For them, there is no alternative to defensiveness seen here as a consequence of an innate, fixed way of relating – rather than something potentially more fluid and related to contextual and other factors that may be subject to some change. Problems to this extent can usually be traced back through stages of his/her development, often including experiences of childhood maltreatment and trauma of such severity the extent and the nature of the parents' problems cannot be addressed in a timeframe that meets the needs of the children and the Court. Their inability to be relational may also be compounded by lifestyle issues (drugs/alcohol) and/or severe, intractable contextual factors like a personality disorder or mental health issues.

b) In this category you will assess the 'self' as not as damaged. The parent, although often having problems across the spectrum, has some relational qualities but struggles to maintain them consistently, and/or under pressure without the support of a partner, or significant changes in lifestyle, for example, substance misuse. Often this parent will need the commitment of a higher quality partner in order to provide 'good enough parenting', being unable to sustain this alone. Personal change or growth on her/his part would not usually be possible in the timescale for the child except sometimes where dramatic lifestyle changes are made (epiphany) and a parent previously seen as 'not good enough' appears more competent and highly committed – albeit with some way still to go. Even here where there is some potential for personal growth the task may be considerable and outweighed by the overwhelming needs of what have become highly disturbed children who now require very special care.

Some chance

In this category, although the parents have some problems with 'self' and social relatedness, it is not to the extent and severity of the previous category. There may also be less complexity overall. There may be improvements in some areas with a significant shift in the relationship between the child and the parent, for example, the parent takes on more responsibility for the parenting role from the eldest (parental) child who gradually acquiesces.

Here the parents have presented with a range of difficulties that at times have been overwhelming for them, leading to serious concerns for the well-being of the children. However, they now acknowledge this and demonstrate some ability to be less defensive and more relational; often some 'workable narrative' has emerged as well as meeting other criteria, referred to in the 'Dimensions for therapeutic engagement' referred to earlier. Significant changes may have been made in their lifestyle (e.g. substance misuse; domestic violence; separated from violent partner) and have already been established with some commitment (though as yet untested), to achieving higher standards in family functioning.

The picture overall may still be mixed with the professionals feeling anxious and uncertain about the family's prospects in the longer term and whether they are able to sustain improvements. A critical part of a 'mixed picture', where uncertainty and variation in views prevail, is to what extent there is now potential for improving and/or re-building relationships with the children in a way that is safe, restorative, developmentally sensitive and generally able to consistently meet the child's needs. In these cases the quality and makeup of the support package is critical to the outcome. Usually in this category very significant problems at several levels remain but there has emerged some evidence of potential for personal growth identified in the 'Dimensions for therapeutic engagement' referred to earlier. 'Personal growth' on the part of the parent must have the potential to be proportionate to the needs of the child and within an acceptable timeframe. The 'personal growth' of the parent, the characteristics of the child, including the attachment and other needs, and the overall quality of the child-parent relationship will all be closely linked, and likely to be central issues defining the potential for rehabilitation. Other important factors from the 'Dimensions for therapeutic engagement' will also guide you here such as 'parents' awareness of the need for change' – as well as their potential to engage and sustain their motivation throughout therapy. Similarly, parents here should have potential to generate secure attachment experience for their children albeit with some direction and/or support at the beginning.

As referred to earlier, the child is appropriately involved in the work according to the vagaries of the case – though I strongly recommend seeing them together at an early stage wherever possible. In subsequent sessions with the parents you can meaningfully bring the child into the room even when she/he is not there. This will, among other things, enable you to have developed a view of the child's needs as well as the context in which change may need to occur.

At the warmer end of the 'some chance' spectrum, families will have already made significant progress but some residual problems remain, such as: developing their own support system; the conflict between the family and some professionals; and finding suitable accommodation and/or school placement.

Every chance

In this category core or fundamental problems in the family have improved significantly. If there are residual problems they are not on a scale that fundamentally affects the well-being or causes significant harm for the child. The main focus at this point is in developing a coherent plan that has contingencies for any setback, which often occurs, and is in itself a considerable task. A poorly thought-through plan, without appropriate therapeutic and other support, can cause a serious often unnecessary decline in the family's prospects – further damaging the children. Sometimes the progress of cases in this category is held up by professional uncertainty and indecision, or the need to find adequate accommodation and appropriate support. Families in this category are by this stage much more able to address the problems of central concern as they arise. There is clear evidence of a relationship base between child and parent in which the child's attachment needs are largely met and in which the parent demonstrates a capacity for empathy and reflective functioning. In many respects the family would now be largely indistinguishable from most other families in their community.

Establishing where on the continuum you consider the parent's potential to be, is the substance of the assessment, as is the relationship between the parameters referred to earlier and parent's ability (or potential) to be relational across a number of critical areas. The extent to which they have engaged and perhaps developed 'workable narrative' in your sessions may also be a positive indicator. Conceptualising parents' problems and potential for change on a continuum that allows for progress or deterioration, is useful for other professionals as well as the court, as they attempt to gauge the severity, extent, as well as the nature of a parent's difficulties. What are identified as the fundamental deficits or concerns, and how they relate to 'significant harm', as well as the therapeutic issues which have been identified, is likely to be the core of your assessment.

References

Bugental, J. (1999). *Psychotherapy Isn't What You Think. Bringing the Psychotherapeutic Engagement into the Living Moment.* Thousand Oaks, CA: SAGE.

Castonguay, L.G. and Hill, C.E. (2012). *Transformation in Psychotherapy: Corrective Experiences Across Cognitive Behavioral, Humanistic and Psychodynamic Approaches.* Washington, DC: American Psychological Association. Issue xiii: 390.

Flaskas, C. (1997). 'Engagement and the therapeutic relationship in systemic therapy'. *Journal of Family Therapy*, 19(3): 263–82.

Fonaghy, P., Steele, M., Steel, H., Moran, G. and Higgitt, A. (1991). 'The capacity for understanding mental states: The reflective self in parent and child and its significance for security of attachment'. *Infant Mental Health Journal*, 13: 200–17.

Kavner, E. and McNab, S. (2005). 'Shame and the therapeutic relationship'. In: C. Flaskas, B. Mason and A. Perlesz (eds), *The Space Between.* London: Karnac.

Kennedy, R. (2005). *Psychotherapists as Expert Witnesses: Families at Breaking Point.* London: Karnac.

Reder, P. and Lucey, C. (1995). *Assessment of Parenting: Psychiatric and Psychological Contributions.* London: Routledge.

Reder, P., Duncan, S. and Lucey, C. (2003). *Studies in the Assessment of Parenting.* London: Routledge.

Schaffer, H.R. (1998). *Making Decisions About Children*, 2nd edn. Oxford: Blackwell.

Schore, A.N. (1994). *Affect Regulation and the Origin of the Self: The Neurobiology of Emotional Development.* New Jersey Hove, UK: Lawrence Erlbaum Associates.

Wallin, D.J. (2007). *Attachment in Psychotherapy.* London: Guilford Press.

Chapter 6

Influence of legal/professional context on parental and professional activity

Overview

This chapter begins by examining the influence of the legal-professional context on parental and professional activity. In particular, it considers the nature of the parent–social worker relationship and how the inherent conflict in their relationship prevents a meaningful dialogue between them and therefore prevents any progress. The sometimes intense intransigent nature of the positions taken by parents – and sometimes the professionals in this context – leads to a discussion about the significance of 'positioning theory' and other factors that may be relevant in untangling aspects of this complexity. Understanding the dilemmas faced by parents and professionals and finding a way through the intransigence and stalemate that develops is then reviewed.

The significance of the social worker–parent relationship

Prior to this study, I was unaware of the complexity surrounding the childcare social work role once legal proceedings have commenced. I was aware of the conflict that develops in some cases between the parents and the professionals – which is to some extent understandable given the nature of the work – but I had not appreciated the restrictions on the social work role that are referred to earlier in Chapter 2 (Woodcock, 2003; Parton *et al.*, 1997; Fook *et al.*, 1997). For example, it is extremely difficult for a social worker to accrue evidence and build toward a watertight legal position, while at the same time supporting the family with their, often significant, welfare issues. Fulfilling both these roles demands a certain amount of relational gymnastics on the part of the social worker, who for their part might also have expectations that the parent will work with them, whatever their concerns.

These are families with long-standing, complex, multifaceted problems that are often the cause of considerable concern to the agencies. Establishing any sort of a working relationship with the parents in these circumstances is often very challenging for the social worker. In these testing, adversarial circumstances the social worker has to be guarded against under as well as overinvolvement in terms of their relationship with the parents. Both have their pitfalls and can lead to a relational breakdown involving the 'personalising' of the differences between them.

In cases where the conflict between them becomes more intense and adversarial, and increasingly personal, there is less potential for meaningful dialogue to take place. Professionals across the disciplines are not immune to personalising matters in professional relationships with each other; I confess it is something I have been guilty of at times. For example, in some of these cases I have secretly 'blamed' the social worker (for a while) who I have perceived as unnecessarily obstructive and actively preventing progress in a case. In the way the research suggests social workers tend to see problems wholly located in the parent, I, too, was guilty of perceiving the obstacles to progress in some cases as located in them – although not directly saying so. Here we can benefit from the influence of the third person position, supervisors, trusted colleagues, etc., as well as taking a reflexive position in our work. I am grateful to colleagues in social work and family therapy in particular who helped me reach beyond the personal and subjective in this difficult area and to look again with fresh eyes.

Holland (2004) recommends maintaining a 'reflexive awareness' of the impact of the 'assessor' (social worker) on the 'assessment relationship' with the person being 'assessed' (parent). She concluded that three main factors influenced social workers' decision making:

- Parent-related factors such as parenting skills and relationships between parents;
- the ability of parents to change their behaviour and lifestyle in an acceptable timescale;
- the verbal interactions (relationship) between the parents and assessing social worker.

The latter was given the highest status by the social workers in her study, emphasising the importance of 'engagement' and the relationship between the 'assessor' and the 'assessed' in assessment.

Clifford (1998) similarly says: 'Both the reactions of the users to the assessment process and the changing perspectives of the professionals need to be scrutinised within this framework, so that the reactions of those being assessed can be understood as a specific response to a particular set of powerful relationships at a particular point in their lives.' White (1997) and Payne (1998) also draw attention to the importance of reflexive awareness and the 'circular process of thought' that considers the influence of the 'assessor' on the person being assessed, but also the potential of the assessed individual's responses and experiences affecting the thoughts and belief systems of the assessor. They each pay attention to the potential circularity and mutual influence in the assessment experience as well as the overriding importance of the 'assessment relationship' on the quality of the assessment outcome.

Social workers and other professionals are challenged in this work to engage parents in their assessment when they are often reluctant and/or resistant to being assessed. During assessments where there has been serious concerns about parents' competence and motivation, social workers depend on parents providing a 'plausible explanation' via a kind of 'confessional statement from the parents' and become 'frustrated and disarmed' when that does not happen (Holland, 2004). The parent's resistance or failure to provide the expected response, coupled with the social worker's frustration with the parent, leads to the development of a dynamic that undermines the assessment relationship. This is a phenomenon often not understood by either party and exacerbated by the adversarial context in which the assessment is conducted.

The relational problems referred to here are typical of those in counselling and psychotherapy that social work used to be so closely linked with. The families referred to here are often marginalised, and therefore compromised by issues of class, culture and statutory power, that naturally influence engagement, and emotional distance (transference) which are critical to the outcome. In a way there are echoes with Minuchin's (1969) work – *Families of the Slums,* in which he joined the family system to experience what they experienced and to connect with them without becoming 'enmeshed'. Here he was struggling to manage the emotional distance with the family, and find a balance between being under or overinvolved, so that he could remain meaningfully engaged and therefore still able to help them.

Minuchin's seminal work with families from marginalised communities is still relevant today. The parents have many problems themselves at different levels; they are constrained by their personal developmental histories, by the consequences of significant events (including trauma) in their lives, and by the pressure of legal proceedings and losing their children to care. Similarly, professionals are constrained by the conflicting demands imposed on them to produce (written and verbal) evidence for the legal proceedings, and support the family and meet their welfare requirements. Alongside this there are additional pressures brought about by the 'risk aversive' culture and society's, often unrealistic, expectations of social workers to protect children whatever the circumstances. The combined effect of these pressures will inevitably have an impact on the social worker–parent dynamics often resulting in more 'formal' relationship activity and the social work role being more 'strictly and rigidly undertaken'.

My research uncovered the views of other 'Experts' who acknowledged how the risk-aversive professional context, and the fear of making a perceived mistake also has an impact on them and how they undertake their work.

The relationship between parents and professionals often changes the closer the case moves toward legal proceedings. Once legal proceedings are initiated it potentially re-defines their relationship as adversarial if it wasn't already so;

any differences of opinion regarding the history of events and culpability is now likely to exacerbate further conflict between them, as the opportunity for 'meaningful dialogue' diminishes. The social worker and parent, often unable to understand the dynamics, become increasingly frustrated and move ever further from a mutual understanding and potential resolution. If legal proceedings drag on, parents' and professional's positions can become more entrenched and legally defined, leaving little scope for relating to each other about anything else (e.g. any welfare problems or contact issues). Parent–professional relationship conflict is illustrated in each of the case study examples (Chapter 4). It is a fundamental cause of stress for the parents and an obstacle for social workers in achieving a 'working together' relationship.

The social worker needs the cooperation of the parents, so too the parents need help from the social worker. For example, the parents often depend on the social worker to help organise appropriate contact for them with the child, and need help with a wide range of welfare requirements (Brophy *et al.*, 2005). Evidence from the case studies indicates that, as their ability to collaborate and negotiate diminishes, then extremely important, often highly emotive issues such as routine child contact, cannot be resolved via discussion between them, and instead find their way to the court arena to be resolved. In this way something relatively straightforward becomes much more complex, heightening the intensity between parent and professional. It also tends to occupy more and more of the court's time.

Findings from this study, especially the Smith family (Case Study 1) and the Morris family (Case Study 3), indicate that fundamental disagreement and conflict dominate exchanges between them. Neither party understands or relates to the position of the other with any new issue raised, resulting in further conflict. A premise of this study is that there are some parents who may have potential for reunification – not previously realised, or that the potential has developed as a result of and during the course of the proceedings. In this context there is a risk that any potential positive changes in the parent would be perceived by the social worker with some suspicion and unlikely to be recognised as a (therapeutic) opportunity. Having also decided that the parent is clearly not 'good enough' (detailed in their written evidence) any potential for therapeutic work at this stage is likely to present them with a dilemma. If the parent benefits from an intervention it will potentially undermine their case, and if not, the intervention incurs additional time causing further delay to the proceedings and considerable cost, not least in emotional terms for the children who remain in limbo.

I made reference to research by Woodcock (2003) in Chapter 2, which indicates social workers often appear not to take account of parents' underlying emotional and psychological problems in their assessments or work with those parents. I very much support this view as it is in line with my experience in many cases including those in this study. In some cases, it would appear that information from psychological assessments has been misunderstood or misrepresented and used to provide further evidence of parents' incompetence and general inability to cope rather than a focus for intervention and/or support. Another concern is that in an attempt to provide interventions for parents but without really understanding the nature of parental difficulties and obvious limitations, parents can be provided with inappropriate and/or untimely assistance. In this context, assistance is almost bound to fail and further undermines the parents' case, often exacerbating further attachment issues for the children when the plan for rehabilitation fails. In retrospect it can appear to the parents as if they were almost set up to fail.

I do have sympathy with the social work position as they can be criticised whichever route they take. This is a real dilemma, as they have often to put together plans for either reunification or permanency, in very complex cases, without ready access to the kind of expertise (psychological, therapeutic, etc.) they need. Identifying families with the potential to be reunited and providing a robust therapeutic and support package, is highly specialised work requiring more than a social work perspective. While I am concerned in this study with families whose potential to be reunited is not being recognised by professionals, I am also concerned when families are reunited without appropriate assessments and robust plans for support and therapeutic intervention, the lack of which inadvertently places children at further risk.

Parton *et al.* (1997) and Woodcock (2003) argue that the problem in the social work role is caused by the conflict created by the 'assessment of risk' and the 'assessment of need', with the former being the dominant theme. As Browne and Lynch (1996) put it 'child protection is enhanced by the improvements in the welfare of families and the promotion of positive parenting and child care.' This is based on the notion that parents' problems are likely to be multiply determined and addressing them will require a range of solutions (referred to in Chapter 2 by Turney *et al.*, 2011). I also consider most Experts would be inclined to support this view. However, according to the research, social workers by this stage are occupied with the legal position as well as a potentially fixed view that the parents need to change and accept responsibility (Parton *et al.*, 1997) for their actions (culpability); a bi-product of this position is that it potentially undermines being alerted to any new developments including possibilities for parental change.

In this context the social worker's role is 'investigative' and geared toward assessment, identifying any concerns for the child. There is also an expectation that they will be supportive to the family and doing what they can to meet any welfare needs in the process (Browne and Lynch, 1996). However, as the relationship becomes dominated by the investigation and identifying concerns, rather than supporting interventions, the parents' perceptions of the social worker is likely to change from one of support (if that did exist earlier or up to this point), to one that is perceived increasingly as a threat to the family. With the parents wanting help and the social workers believing 'parents should change' and 'take responsibility' (Woodcock, 2003), there is an inevitable ideological, as well as interactional clash.

The evidence here strongly suggests that when the balance of the social worker's approach favours investigation rather than support, and where the prevailing professional belief is that 'parents need to change' and 'accept responsibility' (as opposed to needing help), parents are likely to become inordinately defensive. Their reaction in this study was often that of a deep sense of unbridled 'shame' that was not held (therapeutically) by anyone. This was often manifest in various forms of defensiveness and was projected as anger, ambivalence, or overwhelming passivity and dependence; their (unconscious) strategy depending on their well-established response to dealing with such stresses. In other examples in my experience where the social worker can maintain a more effective balance of the roles, it can potentially lead to a more collaborative relationship, as demonstrated with each of the case study examples.

The complex social worker–parent dynamic referred to here in some cases creates almost impossible demands on the social work role, and this has consequences for the parents. The nature of the conflict and the underlying dynamic is not generally well understood and/or considered in the case management. Unfortunately, the 'surface-static' notion (referred to in Chapter 2) described by Woodcock (2003), often underpinning the social work approach is likely to perceive the 'defensive parent' as the 'actual parent', and their behaviour as something that is unacceptable and very unlikely to change; whereas an alternative view would have an appreciation of the parents' context and understanding the defensiveness as a coping mechanism, perhaps hiding underlying psychological and other problems that need to be addressed.

Case complexity of this type benefits from supervision that can take a psychological or therapeutic perspective of the relational exchanges between social worker and the parent, alongside the routine casework management. In my view some cases benefit from external consultancy providing (non-social work) expertise to help unpick the relational complexity and parents' underlying psychological needs.

In my case studies the collaborative potential (in parents) was often kept alive long enough by someone else other than the social worker in the professional system, so that my and other interventions had some potential at a later stage. In each of the case studies except that of Jean (Case Study 5) there was a change of social worker before it led to an improvement in the parent–social worker relationship. The relationship between the social worker and Jean eventually developed into one of mutual respect after a period of quite severe conflict between them. In Sheila's case (Case Study 4) she talks about Martin, the new social worker, who arrived at the point of change and saw her through the reunification process, in very positive, even glowing terms. Qualitative improvements in the relationship between parent and social worker, that included mutual trust and respect, undoubtedly accelerated the rehabilitative process.

In the Morris family (Case Study 3) it was the family support worker who played this containing role while it was the contact workers as well as the foster carer in Jean's situation (Case Study 5). These professionals not only kept alive the professional link with parents, but also appeared to enhance their relationships with the parent in the process. This seemed to contribute to the parent's well-being, but also offered me an insight into the parent's potential to be relational with a professional in the childcare system – if not their social worker. This strongly indicated the problem lay more in the oppressive climate of the professional context and its influence on the role of the statutory social worker and to a lesser extent the children's guardian. A family support worker and contact worker do not carry critical (child protection) case responsibility, nor do they have to be responsible for building a legal case, hence they are out of the 'legal loop' and its inherent pressures, that is present in all these cases. This demonstrated for me the importance of childcare professionals having a better understanding of the relationship dynamics in these circumstances, alongside the valuable psychological literature on parents' underlying problems referred to earlier and in Chapter 2. I do appreciate these are very significant challenges for social workers and their managers in the current unforgiving professional climate. However, if social workers and managers can develop a greater awareness of this dynamic, and understand the nature of parents' defensive behaviour, it could potentially lead to a re-balancing of the parent–social worker relationship in some cases.

In order to better understand the historical role and function of social workers I now make reference to some of their guiding principles. Biestek (1961) originally identified a set of guiding principles for social work practice, later updated and summarized by Miley and Dubois (1992). They describe social work as: 'Guided by a distinct set of abstract values and a Code of Ethics. These values are transformed into accepted practice principles for the purpose of informing our intervention with clients.' The principles are: 'Acceptance; Affirming Individuality; Purposeful Expression of Feelings; Non-judgmentalism; Objectivity; Controlled Emotional Involvement; Self-determination; Confidentiality'.

From its earliest origins it is possible to identify an emphasis on relationship-building as well as a significant therapeutic dimension in social work practice. As Howe (1995) reports, social work principles of 'understanding' and 'empathy' have their roots in the work of Rogers (1961) and Truax and Carkhuff (1967) and therefore have a natural link with counselling and psychotherapy. Despite the efforts of Howe (1995), Barlow and Scott (2011), Turney *et al.* (2011) and others in recent times to encourage a return to relationship-based social work it does appear that practice, in child protection at least, has largely departed from these principles – even though there is a strong argument for a more sophisticated use of such skills. However, I also agree with Browne and Lynch (1996) that it is questionable whether social workers have developed the necessary skills for this kind of approach given the limitations imposed by the contemporary 'risk-aversive' professional culture that naturally inhibits this kind of practice development. Indeed social workers have indicated their own concerns in a review of recent research by Turney *et al.* (2011), regarding adequate training to meet the multiple expectations of their role. In essence this boils down to whether we want social workers to be 'caseworkers' or 'case managers'; the former, requiring an emphasis on close, supportive relationships seeking to directly address problems with families; while the latter implies more of a detached, organisational and management approach to addressing family problems, whereby the parents' relationship needs and any interventions are secondary and often met by others.

There has been a strong case for some time for social workers to be equipped with a range of skills and understanding in order to fulfil such a demanding role. Included in this are relational skills and an understanding of family dynamics. This needs to be complimented by improvements in supervision that provide this kind of focus. This takes social work back to its roots, which required it to be 'therapeutic' at times, at least in approach whether or not it provided interventions. The case management approach implies a more organised and analytical approach to the identification of problems in the assessment of the family. The problem with this approach is that it risks failing to engage the parents at a critical time, and in doing so, alienating them further while exacerbating their inclination to defensiveness.

Research suggests that current practice seems more focused on 'exhorting parents to change' (Woodcock, 2003) and utilising a 'practical reasoning' approach to the work with parents (Parton *et al.*, 1997). Here the influence and quality of managers and supervision, referred to as the 'context of practice' (Turney *et al.*, 2011), is crucial to how social workers undertake their role.

Greenson (1967) refers to a three tier model of relating that is helpful here. Referring to:

> Tier 1 – A contractual (professional); I – It
> Tier 2 – Idealised (fantasised); I – I
> Tier 3 – Authentic (genuine); I – thou.

He refers to the 'contractual' level as applying to many professional contexts. Whereas, the 'idealised' level is fantasised and implying dependence. The authentic or genuine level of relationship is built on transpersonal values with the real 'you' at the core.

The social worker's relationship appears to be very much at a contractual level, and therefore with a tendency toward being formalised and at risk of not taking sufficient account of the relational or transpersonal elements. The parents may be occupied with a multitude of problems and in the early stages at least potentially 'idealise' the role of the social worker, thinking they can help or even 'save' them. It could be argued that social workers and other professionals, including experts, need to be aware of the relational dynamics at play here. It also suggests that the context places demands on the professionals in their role. It is vital that they have some awareness and understanding of this dynamic so that they can be adaptable and in particular 'therapeutic' at times, to meet the parents' needs. As Howe (1995) puts it:

> It is therefore incumbent on those who deal with people who are not coping and who may be experiencing difficulties in their relationship with others to understand the nature, significance and origins of people's personalities and relationship styles. To this extent, assessing the quality and character of people's relationships is basic to the practice of social work.

The relationship between the parent and social worker was often challenged by how parents felt at times about what they perceived were social workers' motives and intentions. The parents in my study had reached a point where they felt that what they said was: 'turned against us'; likewise requests for help became evidence of the parents' inability to cope. Projected frustration and anger, on the part of the parent, can be interpreted as being 'aggressive' and 'not working with the department' (Woodcock, 2003). The evidence here suggests that as legal proceedings unfold the nature of the relationship between the social worker and the family, even if positive at the outset, has now fundamentally changed. It seems at the core of this is the lack of trust between the parent and the social worker. The parents in my study indicated 'you should not lose your temper' (however frustrated you become) and to 'say as little as possible' to the social worker' (for fear of how it might be interpreted).

At this stage the context appears dominated by adversarial factors, where battle lines are drawn, with roles and behaviour very strictly defined by this context. Unfortunately, even if there was some degree of change in the position of either the social worker or the parent at this stage, it is likely to be perceived with some degree of suspicion by the other.

Summary of key points

The following summarises the key points in the process of the unfolding relationship between the parent and social worker from the outset, up to and including legal proceedings.

Throughout the process, professional activity and parental behaviour is dominated by the adversarial nature of the work and the prevailing 'risk-aversive' professional culture.

Early positioning

- Parents need help, but are fearful and become very defensive.
- Social workers need to investigate and assess to ensure the child's safety.
- Constraints on the (social worker) role and (parents') inability to relate

- Parents (from marginalised backgrounds) struggle to relate well and cope in the context of formal professional activity (meetings, etc.) feel threatened and are likely to respond with increased defensiveness.
- The social worker's role in this context is often strictly defined and formal and therefore at risk of failing to engage the parent.
- The above constraints prevent meaningful dialogue, especially in the early stages, often defining the formal nature of the relationship between social worker and parent.

Conflict of expectations

i) Parents under immense pressure and needing help; they are caught in a 'double bind' whereby they are told to work with the department but by now fearing what they say 'will be used in evidence against them'.
ii) Social workers are caught between the investigative child protection role and supporting and helping the family with their welfare requirements. This rarely works for any length of time and results in them adopting a strictly 'role-defined' (formal) position with parents in which they (and the agency) feel more secure.

A consequence of these conflicting expectations is that it again prevents engagement and meaningful dialogue from taking place.

Different perceptions of core problems

Parents, aware by now their circumstances are desperate, and they need help (underlying psychological and other problems) to change, often actively make requests for intervention. Their sense of dependency on Social Services compounds feelings of anger and frustration leading to projection on their part, further undermining their ability to cope.

Social workers tend to perceive problems as largely or even wholly located in the parent who they 'exhort to change and take responsibility'. The potential solution is seen to be in the parents' hands, rather than in professional intervention to address underlying problems.

Relationship outcome

Parents ascribe negative motives ('they wanted my kids whatever') to social workers' intentions and often by this stage see them in highly personalised, disrespectful terms.

Social workers see parents as having failed to take opportunities that have been presented to them, perceiving them to be resistant, uncooperative and increasingly beyond change.

The nature of the ongoing conflict is likely to exacerbate and maintain the parents' defensiveness, further obfuscating their core difficulties – which remain unaddressed and preventing any progress. This leads to a 'positioning' problem (referred to later and in detail in Campbell and Grønbæck, 2006) with each side becoming more polarised and increasingly unable to relate. There is often an absence of meaningful dialogue between them throughout this process, sometimes from the outset. When it deteriorates in this way there may be virtually no dialogue between them other than what is essential and/or that required by the necessary formalities (e.g. court).

I have tried to lay before the reader the significance of the social worker–parent relationship and how a failure to engage and be relational, sometimes from the outset, very often prevents meaningful dialogue, leading to intense, intransigent positions. The many factors influential in this process find extensive support from the literature including Howe (1995), Browne and Lynch (1996); Turney *et al.* (2011); Barlow and Scott (2011); Parton *et al.* (1997); Woodcock (2003) and Fook *et al.* (1997). I can find no real counter-argument to this, though the literature appears dominated and implicitly in support of an assessment approach that is forensic and case management (rather than casework) in approach. This seems to be based on an intrinsic fear of getting the assessment wrong and potentially leading to a disaster. This type of approach alongside the seemingly relentless, disproportionate emphasis on 'assessment', serves to further alienate parents and undermine rather than enhance the prospect of 'working together'.

'Positioning theory' and relational intransigence

The question is how to understand this phenomenon and potentially bring about change. In this I have found 'positioning theory' to be helpful (Harré and Van Langenhove, 1999). It manages to illuminate the intransigence and severe interactional problems experienced in this context between parents and professionals, whether it is the investigating social worker, the children's guardian, or the assessing Expert. Although positioning theory was concerned originally with organizational functioning, the dilemma of fixed, intransigent position-taking it describes is very apposite here. I am grateful to the work of the late David Campbell (2006) in this area, which was brought to my attention by a colleague. It has not only helped me to understand this phenomenon but has generated therapeutic ideas (referred to later as 'The bigger picture') in response to the challenges it brings.

Generally we choose to take positions within discourses, and by the same token we are positioned by others by what we say and do. Davies and Harré (1990) refer to this as 'interactive positioning' in which what one person says, positions another. With 'reflexive positioning' one positions oneself (and in a sense this is what parents initially do) in response to their own defensive motivation.

Positions are taken within a range and on a continuum. As a position is taken with its attached emotions, values and status (I am a good parent) or as a professional (the children's welfare is my concern), the positions of others will then be placed relative to this. The problem with this kind of positioning, once entrenched is that it becomes locked into certain or absolute narratives that tend to underpin the position taken. There is a need for flexible as opposed to fixed narrative at this stage in managing these cases, which only comes about in a sound relational context between those involved. If for example a person is continually perceived as disagreeing, other (potential) positions become unavailable and the individual (and the context) loses the opportunity to change and develop (Harré and Moghaddam, 2004). In this way, discourses become predictable with one side able to anticipate the response of the other in a given situation with inevitable outcomes.

Campbell and Grønbæck (2006) consider that understanding the link between the position taken and the feelings and emotion that it engenders in that person(s) is crucial. They argue that acknowledging people's emotions, which are associated with a particular position taken, are essential in encouraging productive dialogue. The use and content of a discourse that has sustained a position can only be reached by acknowledging and respecting the emotions that underpin it. This, I would argue is more easily achieved in an appropriate relational context and again is very relevant to the social worker–parent relationship referred to earlier.

Therefore, rather than saying things, 'at one another' the evidence suggests establishing meaningful dialogue or what Buber (1970) refers to as: 'genuine conversation'; as being an acceptance of 'otherness' and the key to change. He suggests that in order to make a dialogical conversation work we have a responsibility to be influenced by the other. Penman (1992) refers to four criteria that can be used to describe a dialogical conversation:

1) The talk is responsive to the social realities of the moment;
2) The talk must be open to constant revision;
3) The talk must recognise the rights of the other's views to exist and be taken seriously;
4) Neither the community nor the meaning created through conversation can ever be complete, nor can they arrive at certain reality. Certitude walks hand in hand with the eradication of the other.

The above criteria are relevant in this context as they identify factors that prevent meaningful dialogue and hence how professionals and parents can become polarised. Furthermore it points to a need for recognition of the emotions underpinning the positions taken within the developing discourse and seems especially relevant to the social worker–parent relationship.

Finding a way to break the parent–professional deadlock

The children's guardian is a social worker who is independent of Social Services and who has a key role in safeguarding the child's interests. Their role allows them potentially less conflict with the parents than the social worker, although by the time of their involvement in the case some parents will have already taken a very defensive position with all professionals. However, it is the guardian who is often better placed to recognise some change and/or potential in the parent should it surface. In each of the case studies the children's guardian played a decisive role, in either recognising some parental potential in the first place, or being sufficiently uncertain to allow scope for further Expert (therapeutic) involvement.

Helping professionals, as well as parents, break the deadlock is extremely difficult once polarised positions are taken. The 'early work and engagement' referred to in detail later, is also relevant here. Although more about the parent than the professional, it is an attempt to establish a new kind of connection with the parent that may later lead to a breakthrough with the professionals. In this work it is essential to see beyond the presenting behaviour of the (defensive) parent and to uncover what might be the 'core', or the authentic parent; here there may exist the potential for more relational and developmental possibilities.

With this in mind, I would like to paraphrase what one of the experts said to me one day as we reflected on the problems of engaging parents in this context:

> What you are doing is saying (metaphorically) to the parent – look we are in this cold, dark hole where we can barely see each other; neither of us likes it here, it is very uncomfortable. Why don't you come with me and sit outside in the sunshine for a little while, by that lovely brook, relax and we can have the same conversation.

By almost suspending time, and being in a different place for a while, it becomes possible to examine any existing story or narrative, with a view to change. From the outset, and especially during the 'early work and engagement' phase, the conflict with professionals is omnipresent and you nearly always feel it in the room. In the Smith family (Case Study 1) for example, I had to constantly deflect the mother from trying to manoeuvre me into taking her side in the conflict in such a way that it left open the possibility for meaningful dialogue, at a slightly later stage. In a sense I was working quite hard at 'being there with her' and 'avoiding conflict' – never mind trying to create change. As the relationship unfolds the dialogue then potentially becomes meaningful and reflective. Meaningful dialogue or 'genuine conversation' (Buber, 1970) is the therapeutic key that opens the door to new or revised narrative about core issues, especially the delicate subject of parents' culpability and sense of responsibility for what happened to the child. This is not only directly therapeutic, but potentially influential in the legal process and in the wider professional system.

In my case study examples each of the parents, to differing degrees, reached a point of acknowledging their culpability and accepting responsibility for events that were of central concern to the court. This is generally accepted as a significant milestone by all involved in the case. When we have progressed to this stage with the parents (while there often remained areas of dispute), they were now more of emphasis and minor detail. Finding or developing narrative that was acceptable to all was instrumental in breaking the (relationship) deadlock in each of the cases. Sometimes anger and frustration remained on both sides whatever the outcome in court and in the Smith family (Case Study 1), the Knight family (Case Study 4) and the Bevan family (Case Study 2) the relationship only improved with Social Services upon an eventual change of social worker. In each of these cases the original social worker appeared unable to acknowledge significant improvements in the parents' functioning and continued to be resistant to the notion of reunification even when others, including their own legal team, weren't. In my opinion, it is important to acknowledge that professionals as well as parents can uphold polarised positions and become as trapped by the consequent dynamics as the families.

The context of a 'risk aversive' professional culture, also limits professionals' potential to be flexible and creative in their role, making it less likely they can be 'therapeutic' when necessary. Cecchin (1987) has written of agencies with a legal mandate being in direct contradiction of an 'aesthetic frame' – where 'straddling different frames and maintaining curiosity' is difficult. Along with Kraemer (1988) and Wheeler (2006) they recognise that the context can paralyse the ability to engage in 'therapeutic risk-taking'. The more complex cases require professionals with a high skill level who are adaptable and capable of engaging in balanced relationships whereby they can be both informal and formal with parents. Having the capacity to be informal and temporarily 'step outside the role' to free up relational possibilities is an important element in the process. Furthermore, engaging with these parents – who are in such pressing circumstances, regardless of the professional role, is likely to require something of 'self' to be put on show – not just in terms of engaging them therapeutically, but also more generally.

The evidence (Brophy *et al.*, 2003; Brophy, 2006), clearly points to these families largely being from the marginalised section of our society and therefore unlikely to cope well with formal contexts, such as core-group meetings, case conferences, court, etc. I referred earlier to Browne and Lynch (1996) who question whether social workers have the requisite skills necessary to function in a more adaptive way. To develop any skill, then, by definition it must mean that not only do you practice but you take the chance of making mistakes; in fact making mistakes is arguably a fundamental part of the learning process with any skill. The current 'risk-aversive' culture that is so influential in professional activity has not developed by accident. While the primary aim is the protection of children, the way it functions is also to some extent designed to be protective of agencies as well as individual professionals. Unfortunately there is little scope for error in this unforgiving (child protection) environment in which professionals and their agencies will be held to account and inevitably feel very concerned with their own protection.

Turney *et al.* (2011) argue very cogently that the quality of assessment is highly influential in the outcome of these cases. Here they argue that not only is the practitioner's individual knowledge, skill, and ability significant but also the 'context of practice'. I support this view but would also add that an important aspect is the quality of the parent–social worker relationship. Here if there is positive engagement, albeit with some tension and difficulty, it can favourably influence the outcome of the assessments as well as provide the following:

- A more accurate assessment of the family's needs, including the child protection concerns, as well as an understanding of the parents' underlying psychological difficulty (Woodcock, 2003).
- A means of assessing and addressing the family's general support and welfare needs throughout.
- An involvement with the family that potentially identifies when positive change as well as deterioration takes place, which may be the signal for further assessment or intervention (Turney *et al.*, 2011).
- An involvement with the family that enables the social worker to be able to meet the children's specific needs in a context of minimum parent-professional conflict.

The government has made significant attempts since the mid-1990s to reform child protection services by seeking a greater focus on the global needs of the child (Woodcock, 2003). The culture of child protection and the social worker role as it is currently defined makes this very difficult to achieve.

The incongruity of the role (Parton *et al.*, 1997) and increasing parental conflict does appear to make incredible demands on the social worker's personal as well as professional resources. Finding a way of relating to parents and maintaining a relationship in these circumstances can be very challenging. I would suggest it is the ambiguous nature of the role compounded by the stressful context in which that role is undertaken that is so demanding. My own research and practice experience indicate that social workers often do not understand how the nature of their role can potentially lay the basis for conflict with the vulnerable parents they seek to engage, tending to see the problem as largely located within the parent and their history. Most Experts and other professionals I have consulted agree that the prevailing 'risk aversive' culture is very influential here. Therefore to avoid being placed in an invidious position, social workers and other professionals naturally become more, rather than less, role-defined in these circumstances, thereby reducing the chances of successful engagement.

If a greater understanding of this process could be promulgated for social workers, and their support systems, it might not only potentially influence the outcome of their relationship activity with the parent, but also illuminate the source of a great deal of personal/professional stress. It may also keep alive the professional–parent relationship as well as the idea of potential for positive change in the family, however remote that may seem at times.

References

Barlow, J. and Scott, J. (2011). 'Safeguarding in the 21st century: Child Abuse Review'. Vol. 20: 238–55. Published online in Wiley Online Library, wileyonlinelibrary.com.

Biestek, F.P. (1961). *The Casework Relationship*. London: Unwin University Books.

Brophy, J. (2006). *Research Review: Child Care Proceedings under the Children Act 1999*. Department for Constitutional Affairs, DCA Research Series 5.06. Oxford: University of Oxford.

Brophy, J., Jhutti-Johal, J. and McDonald, E. (2005). *Minority Ethnic Parents and their Solicitors and Child Protection Litigation*. Research Series 5.05. London: DCA.

Brophy, J., Jhutti-Johal, J. and Owen, C. (2003). *Significant Harm: Child Protection in a Multi-cultural Setting*. Research Series 1.03. London: DCA.

Browne, K.D. and Lynch, M.A. (1996). 'A sad day for child protection'. *Child Abuse Review*, 5(2): 79–81.

Buber, M. (1970). *I and Thou*. New York: Scribner.

Campbell, D. (2006). 'Locating conflict in team consultations'. In: D. Campbell and C. Huffington (eds), *Organisations Connected: A Handbook of Systemic Consultations*. London: Karnac.

Campbell, D. and Grønbæk, M. (2006). *Taking Positions in the Organisation*. London: Karnac.

Cecchin, G. (1987). 'Hypothesizing, circularity and neutrality revisited: An invitation to curiosity'. *Family Process*, 26(4): 405–13.

Clifford, D.J. (1998). *Social Assessment Theory and Practice: A Multi-disciplinary Framework*. Aldershot: Ashgate.

Davies, B. and Harré, R. (1990). 'Positioning: The discursive production of selves'. *Journal for the Theory of Social Behavior*, 20(1): 43–63.

Fook, J., Ryan, M. and Hawkins, L. (1997). 'Towards a theory of social work expertise'. *British Journal of Social Work*, 27(3): 399–418.

Greenson, R.R. (1967). *The Technique and Practice of Psychoanalysis*. New York: International Universities Press.

Harré, R. and Moghaddam, F.M. (2004). *The Self and Others*. Westport, CT: Praeger.

Harré, R. and Van Langenhove, L. (eds) (1999). *Positioning Theory: Moral Contexts of Intentional Action*. Malden: Blackwell.

Holland, S. (2004). *Child and Family Assessment in Social Work Practice*. London: SAGE.

Howe, D. (1995). *Attachment Theory for Social Work Practice*. Hampshire: Palgrave.

Kraemer, S. (1988). 'Splitting and stupidity in child sexual abuse'. *Psychoanalytic Psychotherapy*, 3(3): 247–57.

Miley, K.K. and Dubois, B. (1992). *Social Work: An Empowering Profession*. Boston: Allyn and Bacon.

Minuchin, S. (1969). *Families of the Slums*. New York: Basic Books.

Parton, N., Thorpe, D. and Wattam. C. (1997). *Child Protection, Risk and Moral Order*. London: Macmillan.

Payne, M. (1998). 'Social work theories and reflective practice'. In: R. Adams, L. Dominelli and M. Payne (eds), *Social Work: Themes, Issues and Critical Debates* (pp. 119–37). Houndmills: Macmillan.

Penman, R. (1992). 'Good theory and good practice: An argument in progress'. *Communication Theory*, 2(3): 234–50, August 1992.

Rogers, C. (1961). *On Becoming a Person*. Boston: Houghton Mifflin.

Truax, C.B. and Carkhuff, R.R. (1967). *Toward Effective Counseling and Psychotherapy*. Chicago: Aldine.

Turney, D., Platt, D., Selwyn, J. and Farmer, E. (2011). *Government Research – Social Work Assessment of Children in Need: What Do We Know?* Messages from Research. Bristol: University of Bristol.

Wheeler, S. (ed.) (2006). *Difference and Diversity in Counseling: A Psychodynamic Perspective*. Basingstoke: Palgrave.

White, S. (1997). 'Beyond retroduction? Hermeneutics, reflexivity and social work practice', *British Journal of Social Work*, 27(5): 739–54.

Woodcock, J. (2003). 'The social work assessment of parenting: An exploration'. *British Journal of Social Work*, 33(1): 87–106.

Chapter 7

Critical aspects of therapy

The who, how and where of creating a therapeutic context

Overview

This chapter begins with a review of the factors considered relevant in establishing a 'therapeutic context' in work with 'marginalised' families. It considers the value of moving away from the traditional therapy room in cases where engagement in particular, is threatened by the client's overwhelming contextual problems, including alienation. It also refers to therapist qualities such as 'flexibility' and 'adaptability' as relevant in meeting the needs of some clients especially in the early stages. It then moves on to discuss important aspects of 'early work and engagement' which is seen as pivotal to change in psychotherapy. Here the engagement (or working alliance), the affective bond, as well as the agreed treatment goals and tasks between the therapist and client, are seen as fundamental aspects of the work. Once again the difficulties of engaging parents who are resistant is considered alongside various therapeutic strategies that enable parent and therapist to connect. The role played by 'hope' in the family's sometimes desperate circumstances and its relationship to the engagement process is also considered. Shame-induced defensiveness is next considered in the context of 'therapy and being therapeutic'. Here the distinction between 'assessment' and 'therapy' is considered as it relates to the legal context of this work. Finally 'framing an approach' considers the relevance – as well as potential problems – of drawing on different modalities to address complex client needs.

Creating a therapeutic context

Over the years I have undertaken this work in a variety of settings including a clinic base, family centre, solicitors' office, family home and various other neutral settings. I usually avoid using Social Services establishments unless the parents are happy to do so. My aim is to undertake this work in an environment that is convenient, acceptable, and in particular less stressful for the parents. Being flexible about where families will be seen, for a variety of reasons including logistics, can have real benefit in some cases. For example some of my clients can live up to a hundred miles away, which usually means that I take myself and my service to them. Without such a flexible approach some families would never be able to attend sessions. A combination of logistics and cost would make conventional psychotherapy appointments – with the emphasis on them coming to see me – virtually impossible for them. This kind of approach is beneficial for marginalised families in particular, where a variety of issues, including logistics, will determine their ability to participate. The venue itself is also important as some of the parents feel uncomfortable, and even intimidated, in more formal settings. One parent described to me how meeting at Social Services reminded him of being in care and later attending a case conference that he felt destroyed his self-confidence.

Most psychotherapists and other similar disciplines become used to having their own familiar territory where they carry out their work; their own (professional) 'secure base'. This is a concept understood by therapists and most clients and works well. However, this generally accepted notion is often challenged when working therapeutically with the marginalised in particular. As a result I am not rigid about the venue for the sessions and have become more relaxed seeing parents/families in their own home or some neutral setting where they are comfortable. Creating a therapeutic context for work is not a problem providing there is agreement on the fundamental basis for the work and we each have respect for what we are engaging in together. Being sensitive to parents' needs, including having an awareness of the potential environmental factors likely to alleviate parental anxiety, encourages a more positive response in the early stages.

Reflecting on the extent to which I attempt to create a therapeutic context for the parents in this work brings to mind the influence of my own 'empathic roots' – this means asking very relevant questions of the what and why we do what we do in our work. Being reflexive in psychotherapy, and in particular understanding your motivation, is essential to your work as well as your well-being, and can be equally invaluable in the role of Expert.

Therapist 'flexibility' and 'adaptability' are important qualities in this work. It is important to have an awareness of the formal, versus informal nature of the relationship you have with the parents, which may involve taking a step-down in the power dynamic for a time. Once you are an Expert it is easy to become strictly role-defined and lose the innately therapeutic part of yourself. I am not suggesting that Experts or therapists go to extraordinary lengths to engage parents. I am suggesting by having an awareness of the significance of the families' context, and by sensing their vulnerability, adjustments can be made (by the Expert or psychotherapist) that enhance relational possibilities.

I acknowledge that this client group and way of working is not for everyone. I am also not advocating mass migration from the therapy room. However, I am recommending greater consideration for the context of some client groups and consideration of the critical issues of 'engagement', especially for those who are marginalised.

Making therapy relevant, is far more challenging in this context where severe defensiveness, in conjunction with other factors, is an obstacle to engagement.

Understanding and respecting the influence of the social and demographic influences on the lives of marginalised families, and the consequences for therapy, was recognised by Minuchin (1969). He has referred to working with marginalised families in *Families of the Slums*, and earlier in work at a correctional facility for boys from poor, minority ethnic families. He says: 'Traditional psychotherapeutic approaches fit for middle-class patients besieged by intra-psychic suffering, did not appear to help Wiltwyck's poor and discriminated clients.' He goes on to say that 'therapy is not an answer to poverty'.

I agree with this view and therapists should be clear about their domain and where they can make a difference. However, poor, marginalised individuals/ families also have intra-psychic (and other psychological) problems, which may be compounded by the context of poverty, discrimination and/or being marginalised. Like the families in my case study I would argue that the marginalised are also entitled to therapy, but are less likely to access it for a variety of reasons. Therapy, while having its origins and conventions located in the (Western) middle classes, needs to be adapted or even re-invented in some instances, so that the intervention fits the need of the individual/family and their context – rather than the client and the problems having to fit what, if anything, is offered or available. Individuals, who are prepared to engage in conventional therapy, although perhaps apprehensive and anxious, will have taken a conscious step toward a goal of some kind. Marginalised families often live in a world where choices of this nature are a luxury, and not normally available, and to a large extent appear meaningless to them. For them there are often a variety of significant factors that militate against access in the first place, and then successful engagement, unless they are taken into account by the therapist/agency.

Staying with the concept of marginalised families Papadopoulos (2002) in his work with Bosnian refugees refers to informally joining their social groups to listen to their stories so he could learn, but also, where possible, therapeutically witness their experience. Here he recognises the sensitivity of his client's situation, which includes a complex mix of cultural and psychological needs, including trauma. Realising the limitations of conventional psychotherapy in this context he finds himself adapting so as to be relevant to his clients – looking for a means of bringing his therapeutic self, and what expertise he may have to offer, closer to the client and their critical experience, rather than conventionally expecting them to attend sessions they may not understand, let alone relate to. I have been influenced by this approach in my work, not only with refugees, but with families in legal proceedings, many of whom I would consider as marginalised.

Refugee families often have significant (cultural) problems understanding and relating to a western notion of mental health service provision and as a result often fail to attend outpatient appointments – having no concept of what it means (Davies and Webb, 2000). What Minuchin (1969) said all those years ago about the conventions that underpin mental health and therapeutic services being 'not conducive to marginalised groups' in our society, is relevant today; services are often less accessible and relevant to these people as a result. It seems too easy to assume that clients who do not turn up for appointments are resistant and/or unable to engage with the therapeutic process, and that their motivation is questionable. While resistance and motivation may well be issues here, I would argue that, when working with the 'marginalised' it is essential to understand their particular context; what meaning the work may have for them, and their perception of the service and those who may be able to help. It will challenge the extent to which therapists are able to be innovative in order to engage the client and increase the relevance of therapy to them. Taking a more creative perspective will inevitably ask questions of us as therapists, and the extent we can be adaptable to meet the client's needs.

Early work and 'engagement' with parents

Apart from a helpful descriptive account in Roger Kennedy's book – *Psychotherapists as Expert Witnesses* (2005) – I can find no references to the problem of 'engagement' specific to this context. I have therefore drawn from the wider literature referring to problems of engagement more generally and across a variety of contexts.

Reflecting on my experience of working with families in legal proceedings and the problems of engagement in this work, it feels as if I have had to re-learn something I thought I already knew, and had taken for granted. However, I am struck by the tendency still to load the responsibility for engagement, disproportionately in my view, on the client. After all, when engagement fails we clinicians can always attribute its failure to client motivation, resistance, or ascribe some psychodynamic rationale. It is as if we, and the service provided, are somehow neutral factors in this encounter. This seems to me to be particularly unfair especially with regard to marginalised clients who are by definition already disadvantaged at several levels. In this particular context the nature of the parents' defensiveness and the challenges brought about by legal proceedings, 'poses very significant questions for the Expert undertaking the assessment' (Reder *et al.*, 2003). In my experience if the parents' context is not fairly considered beforehand by the assessor then they are almost set up to fail assessments, before they start.

Psychotherapy research in the past three decades has suggested that 'engagement' or establishing a 'working alliance', is a common factor that is responsible for the change in clients, in all forms of psychotherapy (Bachelor and Horvath, 1999; Luborsky, 1976). It places emphasis on collaboration and is applicable to other helping processes besides psychotherapy, for example, counselling, probation or social work. Bordin (1979) considered the working alliance between 'one who seeks change and one who offers to be a change agent', as the key to the change process. Three themes emerge here: the collaborative nature of the relationship; the affective bond between client and therapist; and the client's/therapist's ability to agree on treatment goals and tasks. Research in this area suggested the earlier the working alliance, especially the affective bond, can be achieved the stronger the association with a sustained period of treatment and a positive outcome (Redko *et al.*, 2007; Martin *et al.*, 2000; Gaston, 1990; Bordin, 1979).

Parissis *et al.* (2006), in a study trying to predict engagement in psychotherapy outcomes using questionnaires prior to therapy, found it difficult to establish predictive factors. However, further qualitative analysis of the questionnaire data revealed 'patients who demonstrated a willingness to observe themselves reflectively as well as the awareness that psychotherapy may be a difficult but necessary and beneficial process', had a better outcome.

Bugental (1999) considers how and what we are actually engaging with to be of fundamental importance. He refers to psychotherapy that centres on the actual experience of the client in the living moment as having great significance for life-changing psychotherapy. He suggests that the therapist engage with the client's 'affect' and 'experience process' in the present moment rather than being chiefly concerned with obtaining information and developing what he calls a 'biography' of the client. This implies, and I very much agree, that the therapist cannot simply be a detached observer forensically seeking information that may eventually enlighten the therapist/client; rather the therapist needs 'lived experience' of how the client 'grapples with the central most significant issues in their life'. Bugental's comments referred to conventional therapist–client encounters but seem very relevant to the work with the parents in my study.

Stern (2004) concludes that the 'present moment is a special kind of story – a lived story that is non-verbal and need not be put into words'. He also describes the 'present moment' as an example of 'implicit knowing, automatic and often out of awareness'. The case study experience held a lot that was intuitive and at times more sensory than cerebral, and not always verbal. It seemed that attaching meaning to the experience, as much as you are able, happens later with reflection.

The meaning of what is 'implicit' is also important here. Stern refers to implicit knowledge as 'not restricted to only the rich world of non-verbal communication, but applies to affect and words as well as what lies between the lines'. As an example, if someone repeatedly says, '"yes, but . . ." you quickly grasp the "but" is the Trojan horse to get inside the walls, the words that follow, release the soldiers'. He suggests the same implicit message could have been released by a simple toss of the head. In my case studies there occur 'crisis moments where the usual rigidities are loosened and where engagement becomes possible'. This has not necessarily come about as a direct result of dialogue but is more to do with 'being in the moment', that provides a new experience for the client that may attract and engage them. Stern's view is that the power of the present moment is influential not just in engagement but in its centrality to the process of therapeutic change.

Stern's ideas originated from his study and earlier work with mother and baby interactions. He is therefore able to apply much of this understanding to the context of attachment. For example, he refers to how an infant knew implicitly what to do with his body, face, feelings, expectations, excitations, inhibitions, redirection of activities and so on in relation to interacting with its mother. How, when and at what pace to approach its mother to obtain a favourable response is already stored as a rich, implicit basis for knowledge that determines behaviour.

Flaskas (1997) when discussing engagement in family therapy refers to the 'mutuality of the process of engagement with therapeutic work'. This implies that the therapist can connect with the client's experience in that moment in such a way that the feeling it engenders is conveyed from one to the other. I like the idea of 'mutuality' here, as opposed to the limited linear idea of clients engaging with us – or not. Mutuality places an emphasis and responsibility for the process, not disproportionately with the client, but more as something shared. I consider the relationship problems between the parent and social worker – although not considered a therapeutic relationship – as nevertheless heavily biased in favour of the social worker who can ultimately decide whether the parent is motivated and/or 'working with the department' or not. No such judgement is made of the social worker and how they undertake their role; it's as if their involvement in the development of the engagement, or indeed the relationship, is somehow neutral to the outcome. Leaving the relationship outcome and whether or not the parents engage with the professional as the total responsibility of the parent, appears to me to be not only biased, but convenient in some circumstances. Flaskas (1997) also refers to engagement as a 'continuous process', being similar to any other relationship in that it occupies the space between the therapist and the family and therefore crucial during assessment as well as therapy.

She describes the influential role in engagement of 'hope' and the part it plays in a successful outcome. Here she also considers that the part played by 'therapist openness in relation to hope' is equally important. Families in legal proceedings will naturally vary in the extent to which they still have 'hope'; some having virtually given up by this stage with others hanging on to the last vestiges of hope. Some families will have been given the idea (by their solicitor) that therapy (or assessment) is an opportunity or a last chance and will appear revitalised at the prospect; other families may think 'oh no, not again', fearing another assessment and disappointment. The families who were successful seemed to realise this was an opportunity; there was a renewed sense of energy and determination about the parents at that time, creating a new therapeutic possibility. Some of this energy, and the hope that was generated, can be in part stimulated by the way therapists/experts relate to them. Flaskas (1997) refers to a 'constellation of hope and hopelessness in which we as therapists engage with, often subconsciously, whether we wish to or not.' She also considers that we sometimes engage with the issue of hope and hopelessness by the use of the therapist's self. However, from the families' perspective they will know that the outcomes of most cases in legal proceedings are not successful for them, and being confronted with their sense of hopelessness and desperation is always a difficult task.

Working with families in this context, the issue of parental hope and the therapist's relationship with this issue will inevitably arise in one form or another during the assessment, and later in therapy should that occur. To what extent it is possible to directly offer hope, given the seriousness of the family's circumstances, provides another therapeutic challenge. It is unavoidable – even when attempting to make no comment – that something is potentially conveyed which the parents in their desperation are likely to try and interpret.

Although all stages of therapeutic work can be considered important, when working with families in this context it is the early work and engagement that is pivotal. Without successful engagement there is no further opportunity for change later – with the inevitable outcome for the family. In order to maximise the opportunity for engaging parents the therapeutic self needs to be naturally and readily available. It is easy for this aspect of yourself to be temporarily subsumed in the role of Expert, or affected in some way by the risk-aversive culture that is so evident in this work. Despite the pressures, being able to relate with them – conveying a sense of understanding of their circumstances – will enhance the prospect of engagement. This is not just about selecting the right narrative but more about, joining with them for a while. It also means being prepared for their almost rehearsed script and tendency toward defensiveness. Finding the balance between being formal and informal with them so you are able to convey something of yourself, and acknowledge something about them, is also important in the early exchanges. The parents often find trusting anybody very difficult, especially professionals. As a result, the parents are more likely to relate to the person in the role – rather than to the professional role itself; a role, along with that of many other professionals, they barely understand.

Providing therapeutic work in this context is about finding ways of bringing your therapeutic self closer to the parents' experience, so it is more available, and relevant. This potentially takes therapists out of their comfort zone and may well be more challenging for some therapists than others. Dealing with the parents' sense of shame and defensiveness would in many respects be routine therapeutic business; but here the context is clouded by the prevailing risk-aversive culture and its effect on the professional's activity; and in turn how this impacts on the parent. Because of this, and parents' hypersensitivity at times, it is a challenge just to be with them without become drawn into conflict. Staying beyond the sensitive time so that the 'usual rigidities are loosened' sometimes creates opportunities for new discourse, perceptions and eventually change. In this context you seek to find something of the 'core' or 'authentic' (as opposed to the defensive) parent, revealed to help determine whether or not they have potential beyond the assessment phase.

The parents in my study commented on how I was perceived to be 'on their side'; a bi-product of this related to their sense of hope at that time, that not everyone was against them, perhaps briefly revealing for them a chance of a more positive outcome. Relating to the parents' perspective is also an important element in engagement and building trust with the parent. It may also be the basis of the narrative work so important at a later stage. It is also important to maintain a multiperspective position throughout, even though they may perceive you as on their side at least for a time. This is a difficult but essential balance to achieve. The multiperspective facility will enable you to help those parents with some capacity to consider other perspectives, as well as reflect and examine key elements in their narrative later in the therapy.

In some cases there is quite sudden (apparently) transformative change in a parent that they attribute to an 'epiphany'; this is worthy of further consideration here. 'Epiphany' refers to a point in the case when the parent, who is usually the subject of the professional concern, suddenly appears to acknowledge culpability and accept responsibility for the core problems leading to the family breakup. They also want to do whatever is necessary to make redress and reunite the family. Sometimes the parents' presentation in these cases is transformed from one of anger and defensiveness to that of being contrite and acquiescent.

'Epiphany' in the (Collins) dictionary is described as 'any moment of great or sudden revelation'. It was a feeling described to me by a father, who having lost his children to care because of his drug use and the domestic violence, came to a realisation of his fundamental part in all of this. While this epiphany appears as a sudden change to the professionals and everyone else, it does seem (from my experience) to be preceded by a period of utter crestfallenness and acute distress on the part of the parent; and then as they emerge from this state there is a period of acute reflection before actual realisation of their culpability. In Norman's case (Case Study 3) there was a reflective 'slow burn' that preceded his epiphany, in which he first reached 'rock bottom' while living rough on the streets and separated from his wife, with the children in care.

In my experience thus far the 'epiphany' effect seems to be sustained and most telling following the ultimate realisation and humiliation of losing the children to foster care. Naturally, this revelation on the part of the parent is likely to be treated with some suspicion and scepticism by professionals, especially as they will often be the parent who has previously attracted the most professional concern. They will naturally want to establish the experience is authentic and will have benefits for the family that can be sustained over time. Of course there are examples where the 'epiphany' has not been authentic, or only briefly surfaced and not sustained. I can understand how it is easy for professionals to be cynical in these circumstances – especially when trust has evaporated between the parent and worker. Perhaps because of this, it is often not perceived by professionals as a potential opportunity.

In Norman's case (Case Study 3) and other examples, in my experience the epiphany has revealed itself to be a therapeutic opportunity that led to life-changing individual and family circumstances. The key issues of parental culpability and responsibility can now be available for meaningful discussion in a way that was not previously possible. It also provides an opportunity to reconsider and address the parent's underlying (often ignored) psychological problems (Woodcock, 2003).

If the social worker is often in conflict with the parent, they may not be best placed for a meaningful dialogue with the parent concerning future (therapeutic) possibilities, arising from the 'epiphany'. Perhaps there needs to be a balance between realistic scepticism on the one hand and appraising an opportunity for potentially transformative change on the other. A meaningful epiphany experience can have the potential to be sustained by the parent over time; it is not an end in itself and there is often still a great deal still to do. The epiphany is an opportunity to be explored by the social worker but also by the children's guardian; and even deferred in some cases for Expert (therapeutic) opinion. If authentic, the epiphany can provide a new opportunity for meaningful dialogue between the parents and the key professionals and potentially lead to transformative change in some cases. These cases may be relatively few in number but the human and financial costs of missing a potential opportunity are enormous.

Therapy and being therapeutic

All Experts who undertake assessments do so on the understanding that assessment and therapy are two separate activities. Although it is accepted professional wisdom in mental health that these are not exclusively separate activities, it does not constitute an ongoing practical problem. The issue of therapy and assessment as being separate activities, and driven by financial motives, is openly acknowledged and dealt with pragmatically by the majority of professionals involved in legal proceedings. In fact I am sometimes asked to confirm that I am not providing 'therapy' and only undertaking an assessment. Not that the legal professionals themselves are against therapy but more it is the rule to only fund assessments. Everything else, including therapy is either provided by local services or usually funded by the local authority, who bring the proceedings in the first place, or in a few examples the family themselves.

I have to some extent made an adjustment to this dilemma with the use of semantics – I say openly that I am undertaking an assessment, often a therapeutic assessment, and I am therapeutic in my approach. This is important, as I always refer to the extent to which I am able to engage the parents (concerning issues of central importance to the court) in the assessment. I see the 'engagement' as integral to the quality and outcome of the assessment, which also underpins the potential viability of further work. I do this in the knowledge that others may already have tried similar interventions with varying degrees of success prior to my involvement.

In order to genuinely undertake this kind of assessment, to seek out what I have referred to as the authentic parent, I will attempt to create relational opportunities with the parent as part of the process – what Flaskas (1997) referred to earlier as 'mutuality'. In this, I see my role more as one of actively engaging with the family and their distress, rather than the approach preferred by most Experts of being a detached observer. The intention is to be therapeutic and engage with the family conveying a sense of concern for their plight and where possible relate to their circumstances and underlying distress. You can expect parents' defensiveness and resistance to surface, as well as conflict and their underlying distress.

The assessment phase is very much about whether the parents can engage in a dialogue on the issues of central concern, including potential areas that may form the basis of therapeutic work. One of the fundamental differences to conventional therapy in this context is that any arrangement is not just subject to the parents' agreement but often sanctioned by the Court. What is also different is that parents often do not always completely understand what 'therapy' means, and have to take more of a leap of faith, compared to conventional clients, who can largely volunteer themselves. These families are also advised by their lawyers to cooperate with the therapeutic assessment as it may help their case, which raises questions about their own motivation, as well as their understanding of exactly what is happening during this process.

In my study, parents who had a positive assessment still had some capacity to 'trust', without the benefit of certainty or even a clear understanding of what therapy might involve. The fact that there is still the availability to (intuitively) 'trust' someone in this way may be a factor that separates those parents who still have some potential for change, compared to those who are already beyond this kind of intervention.

I referred earlier to the significance of 'shame' (Flaskas, 1997) as a factor in generating parental defensiveness. Shame-generated defensiveness occurs quite often very early in the child protection investigation and needs to be understood. When not addressed, it emerges as a dynamic between the social worker and the parent each time serious concerns about the parents are raised – in their private discussions or at a case conference or core group meeting. The concerns raised by professionals in formal situations are where parents feel particularly vulnerable and exposed. In professional meetings – such as core groups, case conferences as well as in court itself – hearing others talk about you in a largely pejorative way, often repeatedly, is very powerful. Sheila (Case Study 4) refers to having to 'sit there in court and listen to others refer to me' – 'as if I wasn't there'. Equally as powerful in triggering shame is reading the written word about themselves in professional's reports and statements for the court. Herein, with voluminous detail, are accounts of parents' psychological make-up, ability to parent, mental state, as well as minute details of the most personal and intimate aspects of their life. Included in this will be the professional's perceptions, opinions, as well as their accounts of what parents have said and done – which is often disputed by them. All the parents in my study described this in terms of having a negative impact on them and being psychologically very powerful. They also acknowledged reacting badly to the professionals' accounts of them at times, angrily disputing details and walking out of meetings. Being unable to deal with this formal exposé of their shame and then reacting unacceptably in the professionals' eyes, did nothing to aid their cause.

Kavner and McNab (2005) suggest 'shame can create a disconnection in the therapeutic relationship that prevents meaningful and authentic engagement, if not understood, brought forth and dealt with'. Bertrando (2000) in discussing the importance of engaging with clients in highly sensitive contexts, where shame and other issues are paramount, suggests 'we observe, [as opposed to being a detached observer], as well as listen to gain entry to people's emotional lives – in a way that words cannot convey'. This is what Bugental (1999) refers to in his 'bringing the psychotherapeutic engagement into the living moment'. Professionals sometimes have unreasonable expectations of parents in these circumstances. The parents are in completely unfamiliar, even alien, territory; they are reacting to being highly stressed, ashamed and often feeling humiliated. They struggle to regulate themselves and be relational as anger takes over. They may often say and do things in this context, which further alienates them from professionals.

Given that many of these parents are vulnerable, and come with a lot of historical baggage, what can professionals do that is likely to facilitate engagement rather than alienate the parents? From the parents' perspective they found it easier to form relationships with professionals who had the ability to be less formal at times and comfortably 'step outside the role' temporarily. In this way the client and the professional are able to experience something of the person in each other. I acknowledge the difficulties experienced by many professionals, including Experts, in relating to parents in this way. Many parents are so resistant anyway that it makes engagement almost impossible whatever approach you take. Despite all the obstacles to engagement, and establishing relationships whereby parents and professionals can work together – it does happen successfully. In Sheila's example (Case Study 4) she found this quality in the new social worker as well as the foster carer. In Jean's example (Case Study 5) she found these qualities in the relationship with her lawyer and again in the foster carer; these relationships sustained her and kept alive relational possibilities that might otherwise have withered. Later it was still available at a crucial time when her son was removed and when she could have lost all hope; and it was available to open a door for my potential involvement that eventually led to family reunification.

In other cases it was a Children's Guardian who demonstrated these qualities; in the Morris family (Case Study 3) it was the family support worker. I would argue that being therapeutic in approach is not exclusive to those with dedicated training in therapy and counselling, but is relevant for most professionals in this work. In examples where it occurred it led to meaningful dialogue with the parents who felt they had been heard by the professionals.

Framing an approach

Cases that get to legal proceedings are rarely straightforward and frequently have a long history of professional involvement and concern often dating back to parents' childhood. Given the multilayered complexity in these cases the parents may have a range of therapeutic needs at various levels. Having a plan that addresses the needs is a challenge and sometimes means working with a colleague or as part of a team. It is important to keep in mind that the therapy is aimed at establishing that the parents are 'good enough' to meet the child's needs and have them returned to their care, rather than resolving all the therapeutic issues.

Because of the multiplicity of need, it helps if you can provide a range of possible interventions and approaches, either yourself in combination with a colleague, or as part of a team. This invariably involves drawing from a variety of modalities and/or therapeutic approaches in order to develop a coherent therapeutic plan. Mixing therapeutic approaches in this way requires caution and of course high levels of skill and expertise. Some may consider crossing therapeutic modalities in this way as fraught with difficulties. The approach proffered here, while not ignoring theoretical and technical detail, emphasises the need for interventions that are timely, appropriate, fit for purpose, and most important of all – relational. This was illustrated in the case studies.

Drawing from different modalities that meet the need is ultimately more significant than being purist with technical or theoretical considerations. Barber (2009) submits: 'some skills are beyond technique'.

According to Wallin (2007) 'it is not only what we do that matters – but how we feel about what we do'. This refers to the motivation we feel and how we experience being with the family and their predicament. This accords with my experience in this work where the 'how we feel' dynamic enables us to convey feelings for their well-being with or without narrative. When that affective level of communication is generated and received, it creates a pattern of relating beyond the narrative.

Norcross (2005) outlines four general routes to the integration of different approaches and theoretical models in counselling and psychotherapy:

- Common Factors (determining core ingredients that different therapies share);
- Technical Eclecticism (selecting the best approach for the person and the problem, guided primarily by data on what has worked best for others in the past);

- Theoretical Integration (two or more therapies integrated in the hope that the result will be better than the constituent therapies alone); and
- Assimilative Integration (grounding in any one system, with a willingness to incorporate, in a considered fashion, perspectives or practices from other schools of thought).

Though I have a problem with each of the above, 'Assimilative Integration' appears to be the closest description to the approach illustrated in the case studies. I am a psychotherapist whose primary modality is grounded in a systems/attachment framework but acknowledges influences from a variety of sources, including professional and life experience. I recognise the somewhat idiosyncratic nature of my (whole) experience and consider it has relevance to the families I work with.

Moving fluidly between an aspect of parenting or parenting skill acquisition and dealing with therapeutic issues – as and when they arose – proved to be very relevant in this work, as was mixing and matching relevant interventions and approaches. In many cases, secondary problems such as anxiety and depressed mood were also common, often emerging during legal proceedings, or exacerbated as a result of them and the combined stress of losing their children to foster care. Once the initial problems of resistance have been overcome and the parent is engaged, the extent and severity of the challenge now confronting you can appear overwhelming.

These families will continue to have problems beyond reunification, should that take place, and will often require support and perhaps further intervention at a later stage. It is not possible in such complex cases to address in the timescale every area of difficulty and move toward being problem free. The intention is to address the areas of central importance to the court, which concern the children's safety and well-being and which will also determine whether or not they return to care of their family. This is done in the knowledge that the family will still have (sometimes significant) problems by the end of the therapy, with which they are likely to require ongoing help and support; many families will require longer-term planning beyond reunification so that support and perhaps specialist intervention can be guaranteed. This is rarely the case in my experience and did not happen to any great extent in any of the case studies.

References

Bachelor, A. and Horvath, A. (1999). '*The Therapeutic Relationship*', in M.A. Hubble, B.L. Duncan, S.D. Miller (eds), *The Heart and Soul of Change: What Works in Therapy* (pp. 133–78). Washington, DC: American Psychological Association. 8

Barber, P. (2009). 'A gestalt approach to organisational health'. *In Case Studies*, S. Penn and B. Kenton (eds), *Change, Conflict and Community – Changing Thought and Action.* Oxford: Elsevier.

Bertrando, P. (2000). 'Narrative, postmodernism and cybernetics'. *Journal of Family Therapy*, 22(1): S. 83–103.

Bordin, E. (1979). 'The generalisability of the psychoanalytic concept of the working alliance'. *Psychotherapy: Theory, Research and Practice*, 16(3): 252–60.

Bugental, J. (1999). *Psychotherapy isn't what you think. Bringing the Psychotherapeutic Engagement into the Living Moment*. Thousand Oaks, CA: SAGE.

Davies, M. and Webb, E. (2000). 'Promoting the psychological well-being of refugee children'. *Clinical Child Psychology and Psychiatry*, October, 5(4): 541–54.

Flaskas, C. (1997). 'Engagement and the therapeutic relationship in systemic therapy'. *Journal of Family Therapy*, 19(3): 263–82.

Gaston, L. (1990). 'The concept of the alliance and its role in psychotherapy: Theoretical and empirical considerations'. *Psychotherapy Assessment*, 3(1): 68–74.

Kavner, E. and McNab, S. (2005). 'Shame and the therapeutic relationship'. In: C. Flaskas, B. Mason and A. Perlesz (eds), *The Space Between*. London: Karnac.

Kennedy, R. (2005). *Psychotherapists as Expert Witnesses: Families at Breaking Point*. London: Karnac.

Luborsky, L. (1976). 'Helping alliance in psychotherapy'. In: J. Claghorn (ed.), *Successful Psychotherapy*. New York: Brunner Mazel.

Martin, D., Garske, J. and Davis, M. (2000). 'Relation of the therapeutic alliance with outcome and other variables: A meta-analytic review'. *Journal of Consulting and Clinical Psychology*, 68(3): 438–50.

Minuchin, S. (1969). *Families of the Slums*. New York: Basic Books.

Norcross, J.C. (2005). 'A primer on psychotherapy integration'. In: J.C. Norcross and M.R. Goldfried (eds), *Handbook of Psychotherapy Integration*. Oxford: Oxford University Press.

Papadopoulos, R.K. (2002). *Therapeutic Care for Refugees: No Place Like Home*. London: Karnac.

Parissis, M., Whitley, R. and Ward, A. (2006). 'Predictors of engagement in psychodynamic psychotherapy deriving from pre-assessment questionnaires'. *Psychoanalytic Psychotherapy*, 20(4): 281–96.

Reder, P., Duncan, S. and Lucey, C. (2003). *Studies in the Assessment of Parenting*. London: Routledge.

Redko, C., Rapp, R.C. and Carlson, R.G. (2007). 'Pathways of substance users linking (or not) with treatment'. *Journal of Drug Issues*, 37(3): 597–618.

Stern, D.N. (2004). *The Present Moment In Psychotherapy and Everyday Life*. New York; London: W.W. Norton & Company.

Wallin, D.J. (2007*). Attachment in Psychotherapy*. London: Guilford Press.

Woodcock, J. (2003). 'The social work assessment of parenting: An exploration'. *British Journal of Social Work*, 33(1): 87–106.

Chapter 8

Multidimensional therapeutic work

Overview

This chapter begins with an introduction to four levels of intervention which represents a multidimensional approach to the complexity inherent in this work. The levels found to be relevant in this kind of work are: 'Me and you' – Therapeutic relationship; 'Doing stuff' – Psycho-educational input; 'Making sense' – Reflection and narrative; 'The bigger picture' – The professional system. Each level is considered separately but is not conceptualised as an isolated entity, but more that they frequently overlap and relate to one another, depending on the characteristics of individual cases.

Introduction

From the synergy of mixed qualitative study and extensive clinical practice over a long period, four levels of therapeutic involvement emerged as relevant in this work. In a context of continuing (reflexive) practice, further refinement and development continue to take place so that the ideas presented here remain work in progress. The levels are conceptualised and described separately here, though they should not be seen as isolated hierarchical entities but frequently overlapping with varying degrees of significance, according to the vagaries of the case. The boundaries are therefore diffuse and permeable so that each can be drawn upon and made relevant according to clinical need. The four separate categories represent a multidimensional approach to this work, influenced significantly by the working framework referred to earlier.

'Me and you' – Therapeutic relationship

Hubble *et al.* (1999) suggest the quality of the perceived therapeutic relationship (by clients) is far more important to outcome than technique. Along with Mason (2005) they consider it requires taking a position of 'authoritative doubt' with clients. Mason also goes on to suggest that the importance of exploring the possibilities for therapeutic 'risk-taking' at key times can be fundamental to achieving 'trust' prior to effecting meaningful change. Helmeke and Sprenkle

(2000) researched the importance of 'significant moments' in therapy that both clients and therapists felt were significant and change-related. They concluded that 'focusing and re-focusing on subject material that is emotionally important' to a client was seen to be a 'key factor in pivotal moments'. They also indicated the significance for clients of expressing a high level of emotion toward the therapist. Sheila (Case Study 4) and Norman, the father in the Morris family (Case Study 3) both recalled this kind of experience where focusing and re-focusing seemed to lead to pivotal change moments for them. In Norman's case (Case Study 3) he would become highly emotionally aroused over some issues which in a therapeutically containing relationship was beneficial and allowed the opportunity to reflect and understand his feelings and behaviour.

This is what Dallos and Vetere (2008) refer to as 'felt security' in a relationship – where issues of affect regulation, support seeking, communication and importantly, 'sense of self' are relevant. It is also described by Sonkin (2005) as the therapist becoming the 'secure base' for clients in order to explore and reflect. Building trust in the therapeutic relationship is of course essential to establishing a secure base. The parent needs to feel safe when venting their intense emotions knowing their behaviour will not be judged or held against them later, in some kind of evidential way. This kind of emotional arousal and presentation (Norman, Case Study 3), may be perceived differently by some professionals. They may feel anxious because of the parent's intensity and projection of feelings, and in some cases ascribe aggressive intentions to the parent. This can easily lead to the professional making judgements about the parent and responding in a way that provokes further emotional arousal from the parent, exacerbating further defensiveness on their part. This is described as a 'surface static' approach by Woodcock (2003) in which the professional tends to relate in a linear fashion to the client's overt presentation, thereby missing the opportunity to engage the client, as well as identify and address the parent's underlying psychological need. It is easy for professionals to become entangled in the parent's shame-induced defensiveness and projection and lose the focus on engagement – which is critical at this stage.

The 'Me and you' dimension refers to the therapeutic relationship in this work. It functions at the core and underpins everything else that happens in the other levels. It requires the therapist and the parents to have an understanding of the direction they are jointly trying to move in, as well as the obstacles to progress. The plan, including its limitations, benefits from being transparent and constantly under review as the therapy moves forward and the context evolves. This is contained in the idea of 'therapy as scaffolding' (Dallos and Vetere, 2008) in which by being non-judgemental and engaged, the therapist provides an emotional secure base, helps to 'notice the feelings of others', and 'finds words or phrases to describe their feelings'. Despite the often limited timescale and pressure imposed by the context itself, this may be a potentially transformative change-opportunity for some parents – if they are offered the (therapeutic) opportunity.

There are of course significant obstacles in the form of parents' relational limitations, and historical defensiveness, when faced with professional involvement. Therefore trust is not easily won in this context and when it develops, may be implicit and largely unspoken, especially in the early stages. As the relationship matures and engagement takes place issues of central importance to the court can be openly considered, and parents' perceptions can be tentatively challenged. This is a stage where the therapist can feel as if progress is being made. The nature of this therapeutic work constantly challenges the boundaries (transference and counter-transference) of the therapist–client relationship. This work feels as if you are sailing close to the 'transferential rocks' – not only early on in the process, but also at other crucial times. It also feels as if you are carrying a huge burden of responsibility for the family and the outcome of the case.

When the considerable investment by parent and therapist does not lead to a successful outcome, it can be devastating for the parents and others in the family. It has an impact on the therapist also – though they will have a professional safety net. The families are generally not helped and supported following a negative outcome – remaining marginalised, often very isolated, and left to their own (extremely limited) resources.

Achieving a therapeutic relationship in this context invariably means you will have begun to overcome the parent's defensive pattern of relating; they may also begin to trust you and perhaps others. This is referred to earlier in 'early work and engagement' strongly suggesting it is the most difficult part of the work and on which any future progress hinges. But it also indicates it can be the basis for addressing issues of self-identity, often at the core of these parents' difficulties. If the obstacles to engagement can be overcome then achieving the significant change necessary for reuniting the family becomes a potential reality. Though many obstacles and challenges remain it is often a more straightforward process, especially if the potential for a positive outcome is shared by other professionals. The relationship ('me and you') is ubiquitous in this context; it is the Sun at the centre of the therapeutic solar system, providing energy and potential movement (internal and external) for everything else that happens. It can also potentially broker, or pave the way, for other professionals to engage with the parents, enabling support and other interventions to be provided for the family.

Sonkin (2005) and Dallos and Vetere (2008) refer to the value of attachment theory underpinning therapeutic work with individuals and families. It is especially relevant in this context where it has potential to enable parents to make coherent sense of the key experiences from their background and developmental history; it also relates to the enforced separation from their children – the causes and consequences, and the nature of the relationship problems they have with professionals, including their therapist. Indeed it is the relationship with the therapist that enables parents to understand the nature of the relational exchanges that have historically generated shame-induced defensive reactions as an inevitable first response. The relationship – as suggested by Waska (1999) – who refers to the therapist as a 'holding and potentially transformative object' – serves to hold the parents' fears and anxiety while they consider facing the challenge of what change will mean for them. This is an edgy, challenging time for parents and therapist, as the parents begin to give themselves up to the reflective process that naturally uncovers feelings of regret, guilt and anger. They will be unused to such exposure and will need the secure base, that is, the therapeutic relationship, to appropriately channel and mediate such feelings, while they gradually become more resilient.

'Doing stuff' – Psycho-educational input

'Doing stuff' refers to a potential range of psycho-educational activity and interventions, that is, active programmes in which information is imparted so that direct learning can occur. A series of international systematic and meta-analyses involving over 50 studies around the world provided robust support for the effectiveness of psycho-educational family therapy (as one element of a multimodal programme that includes anti-psychotic medication) in the treatment of schizophrenia in adulthood (Jewell *et al.*, 2009; Lobban *et al.*, 2013; Luckstead *et al.*, 2012; Murray-Swank and Dixon, 2004, 2006; Pharoah *et al.*, 2006; Pilling, 2002; Taylor *et al.*, 2002). This approach aims to reduce negative family processes associated with relapse, specifically high levels of expressed emotion, stigma, communication deviance, and stresses related to the transitions in the life cycle. It is also known to be helpful as part of a multimodal approach to therapy in other clinical contexts including bi-polar disorder (Fristad, 2006; Pavaluri *et al.*, 2004). Therefore mixing interventions that may draw from different theoretical models to meet a range of client need is nothing new. 'Doing stuff' refers to a psycho-educational intervention which was part of a multidimensional therapeutic approach that did not include pharmacological intervention.

Although there is a teaching aspect in this approach it is not really didactic; it is much more interactive and conversational using the client's own experiences as well as case examples the therapist considers relevant to the learning process. For example using an anger management approach the client learns about anger arousal patterns including their own psychological and physiological aspects of this process. Understanding anger arousal as a feature of human behaviour and common to us all normalises this aspect for them. Understanding their own arousal pattern enables them to potentially have some control over a phenomenon that was previously a mystery to them. This is potentially liberating for them at several levels; uncovering new ways of learning, as well as developing insight into their behaviour and how they interact with their social world.

As the work progresses it enables the parent to gradually identify the specifics of their own anger arousal pattern by examining their past experiences and behaviours, as well as those of others who may have an influence on them. In this way the parents build a meaningful picture of their behaviours, their part in it, the influence of context, and how they and others feel and may be affected. The parents in my study had no understanding prior to this input of the anger arousal process; it seemed to them angry outbursts just happened and was something seemingly beyond their understanding and control. Previous attempts to help or advise the parents had not taken sufficient account of their sensitivity and underlying psychological problems – easily triggering reactions of shame and heightened defensiveness on their part. Therefore being sensitive to parents' underlying problems and making the intervention meaningful to them (as opposed to being directed to attend a course regardless of their feelings) was important in its success.

By studying anger arousal and reflecting on the process in this way, potentially equipped the parents to devise, or co-construct alternative strategies to influence their future behaviour. An important bi-product of this approach was that it potentially enabled the development of insight and meaning as far as past behaviour was concerned. This also sometimes contributed to the creation of a suitable narrative, referred to later. In building a psycho-educational approach in complex cases such as these the intention is to try and shape the interventions in a flexible way according to need. This involves negotiating with the parents and being sensitive to the pace of the input, so that they are relatively comfortable and remain engaged. Its success or otherwise is underpinned by the quality of the therapeutic relationship and the capacity to manage parents' defensiveness as it arises.

Anger management, assertiveness, relationship skills ('picking a good one') and specific parenting skills are several interventions used as part of a psycho-educational approach that benefitted the parents in this study. The therapeutic mix is not restricted to the aforementioned interventions as other therapists and different cases can decide to include other complimentary interventions depending on client need and therapist expertise.

This is an approach that requires sensitivity to parents' underlying psychological needs, and the way their feelings of shame trigger embedded defensive reactions, often undermining attempts to help them. It is also focused on finding ways of enabling parents to be more relational at different levels. These are significant factors that underpin the approach to psycho-educational work in this context. Successfully integrating a psycho-educational intervention as part of the therapy can play a part in enhancing the parent's personal growth and development in key areas of central importance in the case. This is essentially a developmental approach that while imparting information to help develop the parent's knowledge base, also contributes to enhancing parental self-esteem. It is concerned with acquiring skills and knowledge but also sensitively targets personal growth and change.

It was an approach valued by all the parents in this study. It was even more relevant in the examples of the young single mothers who, in terms of parenting and general life skills, were already struggling to bridge the (developmental) divide between older adolescence and young adulthood. Here they were struggling with the problems of a life cycle developmental change that was complicated by early, unplanned parenthood. Their adverse social and developmental background had ill-equipped them for the challenges of parenthood in any context let alone one that left them often isolated and challenged in many areas.

The mothers in this study struggled with factors such as: having been in care; being isolated and not having supportive adults in their lives; unstable, even dangerous relationship patterns in their lives; delinquency and substance misuse; anxiety and low mood; anger management, etc. They started off as many young parents do, ill-equipped to meet the needs of young children in so many areas. However, of greater concern was their inability to create a secure environment with strong supportive relationships that was safe for them and their children. This was often the source of a great deal of professional (including child protection) concern. Because of their adverse, challenging backgrounds, especially the dearth of enriched relational experience at many levels, the meaning, value and purpose of stable, personal relationships for them and their children, was not wholly understood or integrated by them. Understanding the value and meaning of relationships as well as developing new relational patterns at all levels was essential for them. This included relationships with their child, their partner (or potential partner in the future) and the professionals involved in the case.

Here I believe some professionals confuse the nature of parents' problems in this context tending to see them through the lens of skills deficit and therefore basic competences to be acquired for 'good enough' parenting. Parental skills and competences are of course very important but are more easily acquired and become effective in a context whereby secure attachment experiences are generated for the child – emphasising the significance of affective and relational aspects in this work. In an approach where the acquisition of skills and competences takes precedence the relational aspect can be inadvertently demoted (or in some cases ignored) in terms of significance. The interventions emphasise the importance of acquiring parenting skills rather than enhancing the parents' capacity to be relational, especially with their children and their partner. Enhancing a parent's capacity to be relational can also help parents establish their own supportive network – an important pre-requisite to reunification in many cases.

The parents in my study were critical of group approaches to parent skills training because it did not meet their specific needs. They often felt the courses were very good for many parents – but did not work for them. My view is that group approaches to parent skills training is extremely valuable for many parents. However, where families have complex, multifaceted problems, and where parents have long-standing relational difficulties dating back to their own childhood, then conventional parenting skills approaches may fall well short of meeting their needs – further confirming their status as not good enough parents. The families in this study benefitted from an approach to parenting issues that acknowledges their current limitations in terms of skills and relational aspects, and seeks to provide case-specific, tailor-made interventions that the parents themselves relate to as meaningful for them. The 'doing stuff' approach sets out to address aspects of parenting and/or parents' functioning but gives priority to being sensitive and supportive to the parents, while at the same time being informative. It aims to create a relational context ('you and me') whereby the parents can establish a secure base with the therapist and become increasingly less defensive.

Case Studies Sheila (Case Study 4) and Jean (Case Study 5) were both young, isolated, vulnerable mothers who were struggling to resolve many of their own problems as emerging young adults, let alone parents. They both had significant problems in what we referred to in the casework as 'picking a good one' (partner). Helping them to develop a fundamental and meaningful 'sense of relationship' at all levels was the challenging task. There were affective as well as relational problems in terms of their own functioning (anxiety and low mood, anger arousal) needing to be addressed. The process of enabling each mother to manage these aspects of their functioning more effectively led to personal growth taking place but was also instrumental in helping them establish a safe, secure (relationship) environment for their children as well as themselves.

In the Morris family case study (Case Study 3) Norman, the father and Jean (Case Study 5), the mother, recalled the significance of anger management as an intervention. At the end of the process they were able to reflect on its influence in re-shaping the way they related to professionals as well as improving their general functioning. Aspects of parenting and attachment issues were also very relevant in all five of the case study examples. Providing psycho-educational intervention is an important part of the therapeutic package and very relevant for parents who have complex, multiply-faceted problems and a history of relational dysfunction.

A valuable bi-product of the psycho-educational intervention ('doing stuff') was that it proved to be an indirect way of addressing therapeutic issues that might not otherwise have easily surfaced. Where parents were resistant to directly addressing some historical (therapeutic) issues relating to their family backgrounds, or particular experiences, they were often inadvertently confronted with them as they surfaced, via the experience of psycho-educational work, in a way they did not expect. This is activity that by its very nature generates therapeutic moments that might otherwise be very difficult to reach in formal counselling or therapy. The success of this intervention benefits from a flexible, highly relational approach and is strongly underpinned by 'you and me' – the therapeutic relationship.

'Making sense' – Reflection and narrative

'Making sense' in this context refers to how the parents account for their past behaviours/lifestyle (e.g. domestic violence; substance misuse) that have led to their current predicament; namely being separated from their children who are in foster care and the subject of legal proceedings. It may also refer to historical events and experiences that have become increasingly more relevant and meaningful as the therapy unfolded; for example, the parent's abuse as a child; their own or their child's trauma; unresolved bereavement. An essential element is the parents' explanation and reflective account of the professional's child protection concerns, which is of central importance in the case. The account the parents offer at the outset of the work will often undergo changes as the assessment and then therapy unfold.

Although 'making sense' is something that is relevant from the outset, the parent's narrative, and their defensive position, is difficult to challenge in a meaningful way during the early stages; but this becomes increasingly possible once the relationship with the parent has reached a point beyond the original defensiveness, and where they can (tentatively to begin with) reflect on their history and the key events, in a way not previously possible. Slowly and gradually – with the support of the therapist – the parent can find a new or modified position, as well as a meaningful narrative that is also acceptable to the professionals. This challenges the parents to adjust (if not fundamentally shift their historical position), in order to review their existing narrative – something that has been stubbornly and preciously held for a long time. This is far from an easy process and is often painful at times for the parents. Their stoutly held (historical) position and narrative – while it was an obstacle to being helped – also paradoxically sustained them through a most difficult time, when they seemed to have little else. Untangling this can be a delicate and slow process. It is naturally highly influenced by the quality of the therapeutic relationship, especially the trust between therapist and parent. This process is often augmented when the psychotherapist provides a positive assessment of the parents to the court following a period of assessment – perhaps the first positive report they have received. Your assessment confirms your view of them in writing – as per your discussion with them – and if all is well the parents often feel more able to trust the therapist at this point. If the assessment is accepted by the court they may well agree to further work being undertaken in the coming months, thereby relieving the immediate pressure on the parents.

This can be a very significant point in the process as the pressure on the parents to fight a rearguard defensive action is put on hold for the time being. Parents will be feeling less stressed and defensive at this point and for the first time it may allow other psychological strategies to be brought into play, such as a review of previously entrenched positions and beliefs, as well as reflection of past experiences and decisions made by them.

For some parents the ability to be reflective was a limited or underdeveloped skill, for others a completely new experience. The parents in this study needed to be helped, as well as encouraged, to be reflective in a way that understood their limitations. When they were able to develop a capacity for being reflective, it became a part of self and fundamentally changed them. It is helpful to understand the parent's capacity for being reflective in developmental terms; identifying where they are now, what their potential may be, and what obstacles prevent development in their case. This was a focus of the therapeutic work in every case. In each case, the parent needed to have a positive experience of being reflective before realising its potential benefit to them. Creating a therapeutic context for this to happen varied from case to case, but by being curious and gently encouraging, this kind of discourse resulted in some progress being made where parents had potential and were prepared to engage.

There was naturally a variation in parents' capacity for being reflective, as well as obstacles preventing its application. Some parents clearly had the ability to be reflective but because of underlying psychological difficulties and other impediments were unable to use the skill; for them reflection had long been associated with uncovering painful feelings or memories. Once you open the 'Pandora's box' that is reflection, you potentially uncover problems not previously known and/or dormant. As a result you may be dealing with several problems simultaneously, including dealing with historical problems such as anxiety, self-esteem or anger arousal – triggered by the reflective process, as well as encouraging the parents to be reflective regarding their care of the children.

Here 'doing stuff' and considering complementary interventions becomes very relevant. Helping to define the nature of the problem with the parents seemed to help them. It enabled them to feel as if they were being heard and that they were part of the process of the identification and resolution of the problems; it related to them and their experiences in a very personal way, and of course highlighted their predicament and the challenges facing them if they were to be successful.

The process of being reflective with the parents naturally uncovered sometimes well-established, maladaptive relational patterns at various levels in their personal lives as well as their dealings with professionals. Some parents struggled to be reflective and made slower and only limited progress to acquire a basic skill; others, once they felt free from the immediate (legal) pressure, became extremely adept, growing in confidence in the safer context and the opportunity provided for them. For example the mother in the Smith family (Case Study 1) and the father in the Morris family (Case Study 3) were both exceptionally intelligent parents with an IQ of 140. For them reflecting, attaching meaning and generally exploring possibilities, was well within their intellectual capability. The father in the Morris family (Case Study 3) had to address the intense emotional arousal caused by an overwhelming sense of shame in order to free his otherwise exceptional cognitive ability. The mother in the Smith family (Case Study 1) was highly defensive and trapped in a pattern of conflict – but once freed from that for a time, and engaged with the therapist, her ability to reflect and reason was exceptional. As the sessions unfolded she confessed to (intellectually) thoroughly enjoying the dialogical and reflective process. For some parents, being reflective in this way, is a newly acquired skill, yet to be integrated and part of the self, and can be a useful part of their parenting repertoire for the future. For others the capacity is there already – but dormant – and undermined by maladaptive defensive patterns or underlying psychological need.

Here the therapy for the parent is vital, but may only be effective by freeing the parent for a time from the immediate stress of permanently losing their child to local authority care. For these parents, relieving the pressure slowly opened up reflective, as well as other possibilities for them. Once Sheila (Case Study 4) was relieved of the immediate pressure she was able to engage with professionals who saw her in a different light. As the context changed she developed self-confidence, which in turn seemed to free her natural ability to be more engaging and reflective. Her ability to be reflective surprised all the professionals and endured beyond the intervention to become part of her resilience.

Each parent had obstacles to overcome in order to be successfully reunited with their children. The parents frequently had long-standing underlying psychological difficulties often compounded by the more recent stress of legal proceedings. They had problems with low mood, anxiety and anger management, which affected their functioning. For some like Jean (Case Study 5), and the mother in the Smith family (Case Study 1) there was an element of fear associated with their past that they did not want to open or resurrect. They felt anxious about the process and perceived that being reflective might expose this aspect of their past, and were naturally resistant at the start. The pattern and pace of this process was unique in each case; once the initial defensiveness had been overcome it created the opportunity for reflection to play its part in influencing the parents' understanding and then later, their future behaviour.

The process of reflection, particularly regarding the key events in their lives, naturally generated intense emotional arousal for them, including anger toward some professionals. The challenge for the therapist, at this time, is to somehow balance a sense of the parents' perspective, and underlying emotions, within the wider reality. Being creative here can trigger the emergence of an alternative narrative, or at least begin the process. The narrative around who did what, when and why and who is to blame can become a central feature for a time. Having established the foundation of a therapeutic relationship, with a degree of trust, you can then guide parents through a process, where their old narrative is reviewed and set against other narratives and the wider reality. With the pressure off, it became increasingly possible to do this and eventually, with them, co-construct a revised or in some cases a brand new narrative.

The narrative is their coherent story that in its way deals with the complexity of their lives. It must address the issue of parents' culpability and responsibility for the events that led up to the children's placement in foster care. This aspect is quite rightly seen by other professionals as an integral part of the therapeutic process. In this respect the outcome of the work has to do more than satisfy you as the therapist – it must also be acceptable and meaningful to the key professionals in the case as well as the court. The professionals will expect some kind of acknowledgement from the parents in their narrative that deals with these key issues. I often quote narrative I have agreed with the parents in my court report, narrative that deals with the central issues of 'culpability' and 'responsibility'. This often amounts to an acknowledgement of mistakes on their part, and taking responsibility for changing their lives for the benefit of their family. Crucially, it also often acknowledges a need for help and support.

The narrative is also therapeutic in the sense that it tells their story in a way that acts as a catalyst for them to begin to make progress in their lives after a period of entrenched defensiveness. The narrative is not about the pursuit of absolute truth (if such a thing exists in this context). It is important to be reasonably accurate, but the emphasis is more about it being relevant and meaningful for them, and the professional system. Underpinning their narrative will be the rationale for their circumstances – the how and why they got to this position, but also what is different now, and how or what they have already changed, and what remains to be changed in the future. This is demonstrated to a greater or lesser extent in each of the case studies.

The father in the Morris family (Case Study 3) said:

- 'We were treated harshly (by Social Services Department) but it was not a good environment for the children.'
- 'We were good parents but I was still acting like a teenager.'
- 'I felt I could argue better than them (social workers) – I was antagonistic.'
- 'I realise now I was minimising.'

In this therapy the empty chair approach common in Gestalt and family therapy can be used to good effect. Posing questions like: 'What would the social worker or the guardian say is the problem if they were sitting here now and listening to our discussion?' The therapist, taking a multiperspective position, can bring her/his knowledge of the various professionals' narrative into the room to encourage debate in order to review the parents' rationale, and generate modified and/or new narrative. In this way it also encourages parent self-examination, as well as conversations about the issues, without the professionals actually being there, and the parents feeling ashamed and/or accountable. Enhancing parents' reflective skill in this way provides them with a valuable tool (Cann, 2004) that if integrated can encourage resilience.

The narrative can also reveal core therapeutic issues, especially concerning parent self-identity, that may have been obfuscated for so long by the parent–

professional conflict, but may now be increasingly accessible. Finally, being able to reflect on the past, especially key events in the case, and then develop a coherent narrative that addresses their culpability and other issues of central importance, reflects the extent to which they have overcome very debilitating problems, and that personal growth has taken place during the therapy.

The 'bigger picture' – The professional system

Working with the family in the context of the wider professional system is nothing new, especially in family therapy (Dimmock and Dungworth, 1983). In this approach the therapist was not necessarily seen as separate from the family and the wider system, but operating in and between their boundaries, in order to be effective. Others, including Campbell and Grønbæck (2006), used ideas from systems thinking to address the problems of larger (than family) systems such as organisations. Multisystem family therapy (Henggeler *et al.*, 2009) is another variation that combines intensive family therapy with skills training for adolescents with conduct problems, alongside intervention in schools and the wider system.

Here, the 'bigger picture' refers to work undertaken in and between the wider professional system and the family, especially as it relates to the legal process, engaging in therapy, and the potential for family reunification.

It is very important that the legal process works in as effective and timely a manner as possible – not just to reduce significant expense, but for the benefit of children, whose lives otherwise remain in limbo for long periods, having a deleterious effect on their emotional and psychological well-being. Legal proceedings are also a unique contextual factor with particular demands and pressures that can have an influential effect on the behaviour of professionals as well as parents.

The UK legal system is adversarial by design. Conflict is therefore inherent and a generally accepted part of the legal culture – though its value in family law has been questioned over the years. In this context the non-legal professionals, especially social workers, have to deal with an unfamiliar level of scrutiny and challenge in their work – particularly via cross-examination, that many find extremely stressful. The pressure on this role to evidence their case, both verbally and in the form of witness statements and assessments, can often have a negative impact on the relationship they have with the family. The parents in this context, fear that anything they say may be used in evidence against them later – undermining any potential trust.

In some cases there is a considerable difference of opinion between the key professionals (social worker and guardian) regarding an assessment and/or critical decisions likely to determine a child's long-term future. This can also happen when new information becomes available concerning the parents during proceedings that may potentially change the case and offer a lifeline to the family.

The 'bigger picture' refers to cases where there is a significant difference of opinion between key professionals (e.g. children's guardian and social worker; or between Experts and the guardian) resulting in enduring, unresolved conflict between them that causes delays in the proceedings.

I have referred previously to the complex nature of the conflict that arises between the parents and professionals that often contrives to undermine a working together relationship between them. This conflict is sometimes mirrored in the relationship between some professionals as the case dynamics unfold in the demanding context that is legal proceedings. It is by any standards a stressful environment especially for most non-legal professionals. In such an intense context, conflict can easily emerge between professionals over the value or otherwise of an assessment, or particular recommendations regarding the children's future. This in itself is not unusual and is mostly resolved as part of the routine of legal process. However, when differences are not resolved and lead to further conflict and the taking up of strongly held defensive positions – views regarding the children's future well-being (e.g. whether the child should remain in foster care, be adopted or placed with grandparents), can become polarised. In these circumstances professionals who are unaware of the underlying dynamics can be as trapped by them as the parents they seek to help. Cases which are already complex become more so, causing the professionals to feel increasingly frustrated with the lack of progress.

While these issues arise frequently, they are resolved in most cases to a greater or lesser extent. In a smaller number of cases the problems are more intractable and critically delay the legal process for long periods. This is a dilemma for the court that prefers some degree of consensus among the key professionals, in order to make critical decisions regarding the children's future care.

Though all the professionals involved want the best decisions to be made for the child, it is sometimes difficult for them to agree a way forward. Here the adversarial nature of legal proceedings inhibits rather than helps to resolve the differences as there is often little scope for 'meaningful conversation' once there is major disagreement on some issue. Inadvertently, this sometimes results in fixed, polarised positions being taken by one professional against another – underpinned by their seemingly different opinions. It sometimes becomes highly emotive and personalised with each party reacting sensitively to any challenge from the other. What starts as a difference of opinion becomes something much more complex with the underlying dynamics taking a hold. While entrenched, polarised positions remain held in this context, it is difficult to generate the meaningful dialogue that can lead to potential solutions.

Although in a somewhat different context, this is similar to the 'interactional polarisation' referred to earlier by Campbell and Grønbæck (2006) and can significantly delay the decision-making process. Given everything at stake it is not surprising that the inherent conflict between the parents and social worker is sometimes mirrored within inter-professional relationships. While this in itself can prevent progress, and have implications for the child, it has a very unfortunate bi-product in that it often contributes to the further obfuscation of the parents' underlying difficulties.

As an example, I was involved in a case where the children's guardian and the children's social worker complained to others, including me, about their respective views of the case being diametrically opposed. Both had contacted me separately to explain their concerns and the substance of their case. I was surprised how similar their concerns were; as we talked it through it appeared to me their ideas for a way forward were also not so far apart. However, it did not sound similar at all when they were in a meeting concerning the children's future. This seems to be a context, where both professionals (who are most definitely concerned for the children's well-being), had found it difficult to discuss matters without generating intense conflict, almost rivalry, which had eventually become personalised. Listening carefully to their views they appeared to be close to fundamental agreement on most issues – there was little difference in their respective narrative though there was a dispute over some of the minor detail – with each of them responding disproportionately to any differences. To me it seemed they were (subconsciously) competing to save the child by their activity and concern – feeling their proposed plan would achieve that aim, while the recommendations of the other professional were misguided and potentially harmful. The disagreement had endured for months, becoming more intractable as one sought to defeat the position taken by the other.

We arranged a professionals meeting, this time with me present, to see if we could close the gap further and reach agreement with them both in the room together. These are meetings, even with lawyers present, that I often consider to be therapeutic consultations. Here the function of the psychotherapist according to Street and Downey (1996) is at two levels. First, to jointly problem-solve and co-construct a solution by finding a way through the obstacles. Second, to provide information, expertise and, where necessary, advocacy concerning a central issue – that is, to act as an Expert. Though it is not very post-modern to be Expert or consultative, Mason (2005) and Byng-Hall (2004) are among those who argue that 'we should not marginalise aspects of our own expertise, for it offers the potential of doing a disservice to clients'. By being consultative, or an Expert in this way, it is also potentially therapeutic in its approach.

By bringing a psychotherapeutic consultation approach to this situation it is possible to influence not only the fundamental issues at stake, but the relational dynamics that potentially undermine progress. The meeting encouraged respectful listening and acknowledgement of the perceived differences of opinion. I was able to highlight the common ground and emphasise the respective needs of the children and how we might best move forward. It meant bringing an expert view to bear on some matters that were obstacles to progress. It was important in this case that the children received clear, unambiguous information from both the social worker and the guardian, and this would be best achieved if they did it together. By encouraging 'meaningful conversation' and being respectful of varying opinions, and the feelings that underpinned them, we were able to make positive progress. This action was effective in finding an appropriate way forward that meant the key professionals now had an understanding and could potentially work together for the children's benefit; also the legal process, which had been derailed for a time, could get back on track.

In another example where there had been a history of hostile relations between the father and Social Services, I brokered a meeting between the new social worker and the parents. The father had had virtually no contact with professionals for nearly a year, resulting in a bitter stalemate that was impeding progress in the case and compounding the conflict and stress – especially for the family. Both the new social worker and the father were very frustrated by the lack of progress in the case and were, for different reasons, anxious for change. There was scepticism on the part of the father and the new social worker that any intervention could work. The social worker inherited a perception of the father as someone who is aggressive and not able to work with the department. The father had felt betrayed by the previous worker and was reluctant to trust the new one. The mother persuaded the father to participate and I did likewise with the social worker. After some preparatory work with each of the parties we all met to discuss the issues, and hopefully lay a basis for ongoing dialogue. We met in the family home and I managed the early part of the meeting intending to talk about anything other than the central issues to prevent early conflict at all costs. The father and the new social worker had not met before but the mother and I had met her.

We managed a respectful, social discussion early on before moving on to the more sensitive areas. I could see there was some motivation on the part of the father and the social worker for this to succeed as we cautiously made progress. I was attempting to create a context in which the historical conflict and consequent fixed positions and discourse did not dominate, especially early on in the meeting. In this way we could, tentatively to begin with, gradually move toward a more meaningful dialogue. The meeting encouraged respectful listening and steered away from patterns and discourse that had historically led to conflict. As the meeting became less formal they discovered they could relate to each other and there was no conflict between them. This one meeting moved the case forward and dispelled the preconceived views each had of the other and helped lay the basis of a new relationship between them. I was able to broker this meeting because of my established relationship with the parents, my knowledge of the case, and the (Expert) status I held in relation to the social worker. I was also someone the father had learned to trust before the meeting took place. Overcoming the stalemate between the father and Social Services opened the way for his involvement in the planning meetings. Also they all now knew it was possible to have meaningful conversation take place between them for the first time, without it being undermined by relentless conflict. This significant shift in their respective positions eventually led to the father's return home and the family being reunited.

In each of the case studies I became a spokesperson for the parents' perception and rationale with other professionals – especially as it changed – in this way offering a window on their world, and hopefully providing others with an insight into their experiences, and the historical position they had taken. However, it is important to maintain a balanced view not losing the multiperspective referred to earlier. Becoming aware of, and understanding the incapacitating nature of the dynamics in these cases, can reveal potential solutions that can free-up otherwise seemingly intractable situations.

Engaging with the 'bigger picture' – like engaging with parents – you must get close to the conflict, to some extent experience it, understand it, and by not becoming embroiled, you may be able to make a difference.

The therapeutic role described here with the professional system, incorporates highly skilled, strategic activity that can not only make a difference to parents, but can sometimes influence the professionals involved, as well as the legal process itself. Professionals sometimes may not always recognise, or be prepared to acknowledge they are stuck. The request for help may come from another source and may be indirect or subtle. Other times it is more overt, signalling very clear difficulties and requesting very specialist assistance. Although intervention with the professional system should be exercised cautiously it can produce very real benefits for all concerned, especially the children, who may otherwise remain in limbo while protracted legal proceedings endure. When used effectively it naturally complements the work undertaken in the other three levels.

References

Byng-Hall, J. (2004). 'Scripts and legends in families and family therapy'. *Family Process*, 27(2): 67–179.

Campbell, D. and Grønbæck, M. (2006). *Taking Positions in the Organisation*. London: Karnac.

Cann, W. (2004). 'A conceptual model for the provision of parenting support'. Paper presented at NSW Department of Community Services Research to Practice Forum, 25 November.

Dallos, R. and Vetere, A. (2008). 'Systemic therapy and attachment narratives'. *Journal of Family Therapy*, 30(4): 374–85.

Dimmock, B. and Dungworth, D. (1983). 'Creating manoeuvrability for family/systems therapists in Social Services Departments'. *Journal of Family therapy*. 5(1): 53–69.

Fristad, M.A. (2006). 'Psychoeducational treatment for school-aged children with bipolar disorder'. *Development and Psychopathology*, 18(4): 1289–306.

Helmeke, K.B. and Sprenkle, D. (2000). 'Clients' perceptions of pivotal moments in couple's therapy'. *Journal of Marital and Family Therapy*, 26(4): 469–83.

Henggeler, S.W., Le Tourneau, E.J. and Chapman, J.E. (2009). 'Mediators of change for multisystemic therapy with juvenile sexual offenders'. *Journal of Consulting and Clinical Psychology*, 77(3), 451–62.

Hubble, M.A., Duncan, B.L. and Miller, S.D (eds) (1999). *The Heart and Soul of Change: What Works in Therapy*. Washington, DC: America Psychological Association.

Jewell, T., Downing, D. and McFarlane, W.R. (2009). 'Partnering with families: Multiple family group psychoeducation for schizophrenia'. *Journal of Clinical Psychology*, 65(8): 868–78.

Lobban, F., Postlethwaite, A., Glentworth, D., Pinfold, V., Wainwright, L., Dunn, G., Glancy, A. and Haddock, G. (2013). 'The role of beliefs about mood swings in determining outcome in bipolar disorder'. *Cognitive Therapy and Research*, 37(1): 51–60, 10.

Luckstead, A., Medoff, D., Birland, J., Stewart, B., Fang, L.J., Brown, C., Jones, A., Lehman, A. and Dixon, L.B. (2012). 'Recent developments in family psycho-education as an evidence-based practice'. *Journal of Marital and Family Therapy*, 38(1): 101–21.

Mason, B. (2005). 'Relational risk taking and the therapeutic relationship'. *Journal Family Therapy*, 27(3): 183–305.

Murray-Swank, A.B. and Dixon, L. (2004). 'Family psycho-education as an evidence-based practice'. *CNS Spectrums*, 4 December, 9(12): 905–12.

Pavaluri, M.N. (2004). 'Child and family focused cognitive behavioural therapy for paediatric bi-polar disorder'. *Journal of the American Academy for Child and Adolescent Psychiatry*, 43(5): 528–37.

Pharoah, F., Mari, J., Rathbone, J. and Wong, W. (2006). 'Family interventions for schizophrenia'. *Cochran Database of Systematic Review*, issue 4.

Pilling, S. (2002). 'Psychological treatments in schizophrenia: Meta-analysis of family intervention and cognitive behaviour therapy'. *Psychological Medicine*, 32(05, July): 763–82.

Sonkin, D. (2005). 'Attachment theory and psychotherapy'. *The California Therapist*, 17(1): 68–77.

Street, E. and Downey, J. (1996). *Brief Therapeutic Consultations: An Approach to Systemic Counseling*. London: Wiley.

Taylor, T., Killaspy, H., Wright, C., Turton, P., White, S., Kallert, T.W., Schuster, M., Cervilla, J., Brangier, P., Raboch, J., Kalisova, L., Onchev, G., Dimitrov, H., Mezzina, R., Wolf, K., Wiersma, D., Visser, E., Kienja, A., Piotrowski, P., Ploumpidis, D., Gomidakis, F., Caldes-de-almeida, J., Cardosa, G. and King, M. (2002). 'BMC: A systematic review of the international published literature relating to quality of institutional care for people with longer term mental health problems'. *Psychiatry* 2009, 9(55): 44–58.

Waska, R.T. (1998). 'Self-mutilation, substance abuse, and the psychoanalytic approach: Four cases'. *American Journal of Psychotherapy*, 52(1, Winter): 192–8.

Woodcock, J. (2003). 'The social work assessment of parenting: An exploration'. *British Journal of Social Work*, 33(1): 87–106.

Chapter 9

Conclusions

The case studies in this book demonstrate that there are families who can have their children safely returned to their care provided the parents can be suitably engaged and provided with appropriate support and therapy. Although identifying likely families, and indeed therapeutic issues that the parents can engage with – while in legal proceedings – is a challenge, it is possible where professionals have the relational flexibility, awareness and understanding. Arguably there are many more families who may benefit from this kind of approach who are not currently identified by professionals either prior to or during legal proceedings, or perhaps at a later stage when family circumstances may have changed. Farmer *et al.* (2011) agrees and states: 'Indeed it could be argued that there is so little attention to it that much of the time policy makers and practitioners do not conceptualise this as a specific area of work.' This undoubtedly needs to change if we are to improve the life chances for some of the most vulnerable children in our society.

Arguably, the need for removal of the children and subsequent legal proceedings could be prevented in some cases where families are provided with appropriate and timely therapeutic intervention and support. Unfortunately this kind of specialist therapeutic intervention and support is often not available in many parts of the UK (Kennedy, 2005), either prior to, during, or post legal proceedings. It is extremely unfortunate that serendipity plays such a significant role in determining the outcome for some of the most vulnerable families in our society.

A key element in each of the cases is being able to appropriately engage parents in particular. This is often very demanding and challenging for professionals including Experts. It is also extremely difficult for parents, who often feel marginalised, to engage with professionals who they often experience as formal, unsympathetic, and with different priorities to them. They often complained of assessment fatigue having endured so many professionals assessing them without actually providing help, support and intervention. The three key elements for professionals including Experts here are:

- Awareness of the potentially marginalised position of parents who may feel relationally challenged in a formal context of meetings, etc.

- Understanding and relating to the parents' anxiety, distress, and sense of shame while in legal proceedings as a basis for building a relationship with them wherever possible.
- Assessing and addressing parents' underlying psychological problems and the impact this has on their children.

A failure to conceptualise parents' response to professional intervention can lead to making superficial judgements about parents' perceived attitude, motivation and potential for change. In this sense all professionals involved with vulnerable families need to be a little 'therapeutic' in their approach. There was much evidence of this in the case studies, though establishing any form of trusting relationship was understandably more challenging for statutory social workers. Here the 'risk-aversive' culture has its greatest impact, contriving to prevent engagement with parents in the first place and then 'meaningful conversation' as conflict and potentially polarised positions develop.

Currently childcare social work systems, and child protection in particular, are dominated by assessments. They are aimed at identifying a 'child at risk', or a 'child in need' and social workers develop the necessary skill set to do this work. Beyond this, social workers' involvement in providing a range of supportive and/or therapeutic interventions is very limited. Arguably returning children to the care of their families requires a different skill set as well as a more appropriate conceptual framework. The tasks of assessing the suitability of a child returning home, providing therapeutic intervention and family support, and identifying and addressing parents' underlying psychological problems, will be unfamiliar territory for the majority of statutory social workers. This is understandable as so few children are successfully returned to their parents' care for social workers to have had experience. It is highly likely in these circumstances that the majority of social workers, or indeed the social work systems as they are at present, will not be equipped to undertake specialist work of this kind. Perhaps this, along with therapeutic social work, is an area of sub-speciality in social work that needs to be resurrected and developed.

Having reached the end of this book, I am struck by the significance of serendipity in all of this. In the first chapter I referred to it being influential in my development – firstly as a therapist, and later as an Expert. To aspiring Experts, especially those who are psychotherapists, it is important to understand aspects of your personal and professional development that influence potential bias, idiosyncrasies, as well as your motivation – all influential in your self-identity in this role. This self-awareness helps to deal with the conflict inherent in the roles as well as the many challenges you are likely to be confronted with.

Serendipity plays an influential role in the life of the families; children are occasionally returned home to their parents, or may be placed in kinship care. They may be separated from siblings and placed in long-term foster care or adopted. Some children still have very significant problems and endure a succession of placement breakdowns without settling and experiencing stability for any significant period. Key decisions affecting their lives all hinge on professionals' assessments, which are pivotal at this time, with much hinging on professional judgement. In the absence of an appropriate conceptual framework in this work, there is scope for subjectivity, and therefore chance to be disproportionately influential in the outcome. This is an extremely important issue, particularly for policy makers, as the potential human and financial cost in these cases is enormous.

Despite pointing to serious flaws in the legal/professional system I have no doubt that the vast majority of professionals undertake their work with the best of intentions – all wanting to do what is best for the child. At times the system seems to defeat itself, frustrating both families and professionals in the process. Identifying and agreeing the best solution for the child becomes challenging in a context that finds 'meaningful conversation' between professionals and parents – and sometimes between professionals themselves – more elusive as conflict and polarised positions develop. This is undoubtedly compounded by the adversarial legal system we have in this country, which is often found to be completely unsuitable for resolving complex family situations. As Kennedy (2005) points out, we would do well to look at other countries' approaches to the same problem, particularly in France, where more family-sensitive approaches have been integrated into their legal framework.

Psychotherapists have much to offer in the context of childcare legal proceedings in providing assessments, and intervention where there is therapeutic potential. I would also argue that in some cases they may contribute to untangling the conflict-ridden legal process that has led to unnecessary delay, in many cases negatively impacting on the children. Although they are not currently on the government's list of approved Experts there is no doubt that in the most complex cases a psychotherapy assessment can be beneficial – especially where potentially life-changing decisions regarding a parent's therapeutic potential will be made.

In my view this is psychotherapy on the edge. It demands adaptability and flexibility on the part of the therapist who may have to be prepared to work away from the security of their therapy room. I acknowledge this is not for everyone and the inherent conflict in the roles (Expert and psychotherapist), and the inevitable compromises to be made, will be more of an obstacle for some than others. At present the system does not make it easy for psychotherapists who have the skills and inclination to work in this area, to undertake the work. However, the attraction for psychotherapists, and indeed agencies should they decide to fund therapeutic intervention, is the potential for transformative change in some cases.

The 'working framework' presented in Chapter 5 offers a conceptual way forward in this work. It identifies key areas for consideration during the therapeutic assessment including: defining the nature of various forms of parents' defensiveness; identifying dimensions of therapeutic engagement; and describing parent and parenting characteristics. Finally formulating an assessment helps the assessor navigate a route toward a conclusion whereby parents can be considered as having: no chance; some chance; or every chance of engaging in therapy so as to be rehabilitated with their children.

This framework may be beneficial in work with similar families who have not yet embarked on legal proceedings, or with families who have been separated for some time after legal proceedings have completed, and where family circumstances may have improved, making rehabilitation viable. It has already benefitted several small-scale therapeutic projects (domestic violence and substance misuse) where there are similar issues related to the viability of therapeutic assessment and intervention. It has particular relevance for marginalised families in other settings where issues of relational disadvantage in a context of formal professional activity may prevent them engaging appropriately with agencies.

Unfortunately marginalised groups are often conveniently ignored and occasionally pilloried by society and most institutions. It is ironic that those arguably most vulnerable in our society find it so difficult to access the services that may help them. Psychotherapy, because of its inherent conservatism, and its roots in middle-class conventions, is often a long way from those who arguably need it most. Psychotherapy is not a solution to poverty, or factors that lead to the marginalisation of some families compared to others; though poverty, or being marginalised, should not exclude them accessing therapeutic help. I have argued it is more a question of understanding the client's context, addressing the significant obstacles that prevent meaningful engagement, shaking loose the usual conventions, and meeting the challenges in a creative fashion. This often means therapists adapting more to the client's contextual needs and bringing your therapeutic service closer to them – a significant reversal of the usual psychotherapy trend.

References

Farmer, E.R.G., Sturgess, W., O'Neill, T. and Wijedasa, D. (2011). *Achieving Successful Returns From Care: What Makes Reunification Work?* London: BAAF. ISBN 978 1 907585 25 8

Kennedy, R. (2005). *Psychotherapists as Expert Witnesses: Families at Breaking Point.* London: Karnac.

Index

For Product Safety Concerns and Information please contact our EU representative GPSR@taylorandfrancis.com
Taylor & Francis Verlag GmbH, Kaufingerstraße 24, 80331 München, Germany

www.ingramcontent.com/pod-product-compliance
Ingram Content Group UK Ltd.
Pitfield, Milton Keynes, MK11 3LW, UK
UKHW011016180926
475701UK00004B/769

* 9 7 8 0 8 1 5 3 5 8 4 6 6 *